Bedtime Bible Stories

Illustrated by
BRUNO FROST

WHITMAN PUBLISHING COMPANY

RACINE, WISCONSIN

CONTENTS

In the Beginning

Long, long ago, so very long ago that no one can think how long it was, there was no beautiful world. There was no bright shining sun. There were no twinkling stars. There was no round yellow moon. There was only God.

Long, long ago, so very long ago that no one can think how long it was, there were no birds and beasts. There were no fish. There were no animals of any kind. There was only God.

Long, long ago, so very long ago that no one can think how long it was, there were no people. There were no mothers and fathers. There were no brothers and sisters. There were no little children. There was only God.

Even before the beginning of things there was God.

Then, in the beginning, God made the heaven and the earth. All was dark and still.

God spoke. "Let there be light," God said, and there was light. And God called the light Day, and the darkness he called Night. God made two great lights. He made the sun to give bright, warm light in the daytime. He made the round, yellow moon to give soft light in the nighttime. He made the stars, too, the twinkling stars that shine in the dark sky.

God made water, and God made land. He gathered the waters together and called them Seas. And the dry land he called Earth.

And God said, "Let the earth bring forth grass with seed. Let there be fruit trees with fruit and with seed." And it was so. There was grass with seed. There were fruit trees with fruit and seed. And God saw that it was good.

And God said, "Let the waters bring forth fish and great whales. Let there be birds and fowl and all kinds of living things that fly." And it was so.

And God said, "Let the earth bring forth living

creatures of all kinds. Let there be cattle and horses and dogs and cats. Let there be chickens and turkeys. Let there be beasts of the field and creeping things."

So God made living things—the animals, the cows and the sheep, and the slow, quiet things that creep about on the earth.

And God said, "Let there be people that are like us. They shall rule over the fish of the sea and over the birds of the air, over the cattle and over all creeping things of the earth."

God made people to be like him. God made man, and he made woman. The man God called Adam, and the woman he called Eve.

And God saw everything that he had made. And behold, it was very good.

This is the very first story in the Bible. It is the story of long, long ago. If you look at the first chapter of the book of Genesis, you will find these words:

"In the beginning God created the heaven and the earth."

The Boat Noah Built

Once upon a time there was a wise old man whose name was Noah. Noah was more than five hundred years old. Now in the days of Noah most of the people were very bad. They spent their days thinking of bad things to do, and God was grieved because they loved evil rather than good.

Noah was a good man. Every day he tried to do the things that are right. Every day he prayed to God. He thanked God for taking care of him and his family. He asked God to help him do right things.

One day God spoke to Noah. "A great flood is coming," God told Noah. "It will destroy all living things in the whole earth."

Noah listened to hear what God wanted him to do.

"Make an ark boat of gopher wood," God commanded Noah. "Make it tight and rub it with pitch inside and outside. Make the ark long, and wide, and high, and divide it into three storeys.

Make a window and make a door. When the great flood comes, you may go into the ark—you, Noah, and your wife and your sons and your sons' wives. Take with you into the ark two of every kind of animal, two of every kind of cattle, two of every kind of bird, and two of every kind of creeping thing. Take all these living things that you may keep them alive. Take plenty of food with you that all may be cared for in the ark boat you will build."

Noah set to work. With his sons he built the ark of gopher wood. He made it just as long and just as wide and just as high as God had commanded. He made a window and a door. When the great boat was finished Noah rubbed it inside and out with pitch so that the water could not come in.

How Noah's neighbors must have laughed as day by day he labored over the great boat! There were no machines such as men use today in building great ships. The tools were simple, and the work took a long, long time.

"Why does Noah work so hard on that strange boat?" people often asked.

And Noah's answer was always the same. "I

am doing the thing which God has commanded."

Days went by, days and weeks and months, and even years.

One day God spoke to Noah again.

"Come into the ark with your family," God said. "After seven more days the great rain will begin. For forty days and nights there will be a great rain upon the earth. Then will there be the great flood."

Again Noah did just as God commanded. He and his wife went into the ark. They took with them their three sons, Shem, Ham, and Japheth. They took their sons' wives, too.

And into the ark Noah took two of every kind of animal, two of every kind of cattle, two of every kind of bird, and two of every kind of creeping thing. He took all these living things together with food that they might eat while they were in the ark.

The door was shut, and Noah and his family waited. One day they waited, two days, three days they waited, four days, five days, six days, seven days. It was a week before the rain began to fall. Then it rained all day. It rained all night. It kept on raining. For forty days and forty nights the great rain fell.

The waters rose. They covered the low places first, then the high places. The waters covered the grass and the trees. The waters covered the valleys and the hills and even the tall mountains. But safe on top of the water floated the ark boat God had told Noah to make.

For one hundred and fifty days the waters kept rising. There was no dry land to be seen. Upon the whole earth there were no living things except Noah and his wife and his sons and his sons' wives and the animals which they had taken with them into the ark.

Then one day God sent a great wind. Slowly, oh, so slowly the water began to go away. On the seventeenth day of the seventh month the ark came to rest on Mount Ararat.

Slowly, oh, so slowly the waters went away. On the tenth day of the tenth month the tops of the mountains could be seen. Still Noah waited.

Slowly, oh, so slowly the water went down. When forty more days had passed, Noah opened the window of the ark and sent out a dove. The dove could find not even a small branch of a tree to light on. She returned to the ark. Noah

opened the window and put out his hand. The dove rested on Noah's hand, and he took her into the ark.

One day Noah waited. Two days, three days, four days, five days, six days, seven days passed. On the seventh day Noah sent out the dove again. This time when she came back, she carried in her beak the green leaf of an olive tree. Thus Noah knew the treetops were showing again.

Again Noah waited seven days. Then he sent out the dove once more. When she did not come back, Noah knew that the waters had gone away and that there was dry land where a bird might rest.

Still Noah waited. It was another month before the earth was dried from the great flood which had covered it. Then God spoke again to Noah.

"Go forth out of the ark," God commanded. "Take with you your family—your wife, your sons, and their wives. Take with you every living thing that is in the ark—the birds, the cattle, and the creeping things."

Noah did just as God said. He and his family came out of the ark. They brought out all the living things that were in the ark. And Noah built an altar and gave thanks to God for his care during the long flood.

And God was pleased with Noah. He gave him a promise:

> *While the earth remaineth,*
> *Seedtime and harvest,*
> *And cold and heat,*
> *And summer and winter,*
> *And day and night,*
> *Shall not cease.*

God gave Noah another promise, too. It is the promise that never again will a great flood destroy all living creatures from the earth. And God gave Noah a sign of this promise.

"I do set my bow in the clouds," God told Noah. "You will find it there after rain. When you see the rainbow in the sky you must always remember my promise that never again will the waters rise to become a flood to destroy all living things."

Whenever Noah and his family saw the rainbow colors in the sky, they must have remembered the promise. Every time they looked at the rainbow, they must have thanked God for his care.

Joseph of Canaan

Ever since he could remember, Joseph had loved the tales about his great-grandfather Abraham. He never tired of hearing Father Jacob tell of the time when God first spoke to Grandfather Abraham and gave him the promise, "I will make of thee a great nation, and I will bless thee, and make thy name great; and thou shalt be a blessing."

"And God led Great-Grandfather Abraham to this very land," Father Jacob said.

"Did God ever speak to you?" young Joseph must have asked his father.

And perhaps Jacob would tell of the lonely night at Bethel and the promise, "I am with thee, and will keep thee in all places whither thou goest. In thee and in thy seed shall all the families of the earth be blessed."

How it was to come about that the family of Jacob should be a blessing to people even in strange lands Joseph did not know, but he liked the flavor of greatness in the words.

Of all his twelve sons, old Jacob loved Joseph best. Perhaps it was because Joseph looked so much like his mother Rachel. Perhaps it was because this one of all his boys seemed best to understand his father. Jacob was always doing things to show the boy how much he loved him. When Joseph was seventeen, Jacob gave him a splendid coat of many colors, a coat finer than any of the other boys had ever had.

Joseph's brothers were envious. They were always teasing Joseph. They could not "speak peaceably unto him."

One day Joseph dreamed a dream. It was such a grand dream that he just had to tell it.

"Listen," he begged his brothers, "hear the dream which I have dreamed."

Unwillingly the brothers listened.

"We were binding sheaves of grain in the field, my brothers," Joseph said, "and lo, my sheaf of grain stood up tall and straight, and your sheaves of grain gathered around and bowed to my sheaf."

"What!" shouted the brothers. "Do you think you will some day rule over us?" And they hated Joseph both for his dream and for his words.

But Joseph could not keep quiet. Again he dreamed a dream. Again he told it to his brothers.

"Behold, I have dreamed another dream," Joseph announced. "In this dream the sun and the moon and eleven stars bowed before me."

Even Jacob was amazed. "What is this that you have dreamed?" he scolded Joseph. "Shall I and your mother and your brothers some day bow down before you?"

But in his heart old Jacob was very proud of Joseph's dreams.

One day the brothers of Joseph were feeding their father's sheep in Shechem. They must have been away from home for some time, for Jacob was worrying about them.

"Joseph," he called.

Joseph came running. "Here I am," he said.

"Are your brothers feeding the flocks in Shechem?" Jacob asked.

"They are, sir."

Jacob put his hand on the boy's shoulder. "Go," he said, "see if all is well with your brothers and with the flocks. Bring me word."

Joseph set out. Down the valley of Hebron he went to Shechem, but not a brother or a sheep

could he find. As he searched for them, he met a man.

"What are you looking for?" asked the man.

"My brothers," Joseph answered. "Can you tell me where they are feeding their flocks?"

The man nodded. "They have left here," he said. "I heard them say they were going to Dothan."

So Joseph set out for Dothan.

His brothers saw the bright colors of the hated coat when Joseph was far away.

"Look, it is the dreamer coming," they said to each other. "Let us get rid of him. Let us kill him and throw him into this deep pit. We can say that a wild beast ate him. That will be the end of all those dreams of his."

The brothers nodded—most of them. Then Reuben spoke. "Let us not kill him. Let us throw him into the pit," he said.

The others agreed, and Reuben slipped away to think out a plan to rescue Joseph and take him back home.

Joseph was nearer now. The brothers jumped on him as soon as he reached the spot where they were. First they stripped off the beautiful coat of many colors that old Jacob had given his son. In spite of Joseph's pleadings, they cast him into the empty pit without food or water. Then they, themselves, sat down to eat.

Joseph could smell the bread and dates as he lay deep down in the pit. He was hungry from his long walk, but he hardly knew that, for he was afraid.

Suddenly Joseph smelled a new odor, the odor of spices. He heard the slow pad, pad, pad of camels' feet in the sand.

The spice merchants! Joseph had watched many times as the long caravans loaded with balm and myrrh and all kinds of spices made their way down to the land of Egypt. In his mind Joseph could see them now—the camels, the Ishmaelite drivers, and the great bags of sweet-smelling spices. He could hear the tinkle of camel bells.

Then Joseph heard the voice of his brother Judah.

"What good will it do us to kill our brother?" Judah asked. "Let us rather sell him to these Ishmaelites."

The brothers agreed. They lifted Joseph up out of the pit and sold him to the spice merchants for twenty pieces of silver.

When Reuben came back to the pit to rescue Joseph, there was no one in sight.

In the home of old Jacob there was great sorrow that night. The brothers of Joseph had killed a goat. In the goat's blood they had dipped the beautiful many-colored coat of Joseph.

"See," they told their father, "see this coat we have found. Is it your son's coat?"

Old Jacob was brokenhearted. "It is indeed my son's coat," he sobbed. "A wild beast has eaten him." And day after day Jacob mourned for Joseph.

Far down on the road to Egypt a caravan of Ishmaelites went on its slow way. They carried balm and myrrh and spices to sell to the highest bidders. They carried, too, young Joseph of Canaan to be sold as a slave in a strange land.

In a Strange Land

At last the caravan of Ishmaelites reached Egypt. Leisurely the merchants traded their spices. Then they made their way to the slave market. For the first time in his life young Joseph saw men and women bought and sold. He watched the price of each slave as it was counted out.

Someone pushed Joseph up the steps to the slave block, and he heard the bidding begin.

Deep within himself, Joseph heard something else, too. From far away, out of the long ago, he heard the words of the promise which God had given his father Jacob, "I am with thee, and will keep thee in all places whither thou goest."

"In all places—even in Egypt!" Joseph dared think. He lifted his eyes and threw back his shoulders. He heard the voice of the auctioneer, "Sold to Potiphar, an officer of Pharaoh's, and captain of the guard." Joseph was a slave.

In Potiphar's house Joseph did his work well. His master's family liked him, and Joseph prospered, for "the Lord was with him." Soon Potiphar made Joseph overseer over all his house and over all that he had. So prosperous was Potiphar that the Bible tells us:

The Lord blessed the Egyptian's house
For Joseph's sake;
And the blessing of the Lord was upon
all that he had
In the house, and in the field.

Things were going well for Joseph, even though he was a slave in Egypt. Then one day Potiphar's wife told him a false story about Joseph. And Joseph's master believed the story and put him into prison, a deep dungeon where the king's prisoners were kept.

But even in prison Joseph remembered the promise, "I am with thee, and will keep thee in all places."

And the Lord was with Joseph.

Because Joseph was cheerful and did his work well, the keeper of the prison grew to like him. He put Joseph in charge of the other prisoners.

One day two new prisoners were cast into the dungeon, King Pharaoh's butler and his baker. They were put in Joseph's charge. He cared for them and was kind to them.

One morning Joseph found the king's butler and baker very sad. "What is the matter?" Joseph asked.

"We have dreamed a dream," the two men explained, "and there is no one to tell us what it means."

"My God knows all things," Joseph explained to the two men. "Tell me your dreams."

The king's chief butler told his dream first. "In my dream," the chief butler said, "I saw a new vine. On the vine were three branches. These branches budded and blossomed, and the clusters brought forth ripe grapes. I had Pharaoh's cup in my hand just as I used to hold it. I took the new grapes from the vine and pressed them into Pharaoh's cup, and gave the cup to Pharaoh, the king."

"The three branches you saw in your dream are three days," Joseph told the king's butler. "In three days Pharaoh will take you out of prison and give you back your position as his cupbearer. You shall wait on him just as you did before."

Joseph waited a moment.

"When things go well with you again, I hope

you will remember me. I was brought here from my own country far away. I have done nothing wrong that I should be put in prison."

"I also had a dream," the chief baker interrupted. "In my dream I had three white baskets on my head. In the top basket were all kinds of sweet cakes for Pharaoh, and the birds came and ate the cakes from the basket on my head."

Joseph spoke slowly. "The three baskets are three days," he told the chief baker. "In three days Pharaoh will hang you."

One day went by. Two days went by. The third day was Pharaoh's birthday, and Pharaoh gave all his servants a great feast. And he restored the chief butler to his old job, so that he handed Pharaoh his cup just as he had done before. But the chief baker Pharaoh hanged, just as Joseph had said.

Now the chief butler forgot Joseph. Days went by and he made no effort to help him. Weeks passed, months, and more months. Joseph had been in prison for two years.

Then, one night, King Pharaoh dreamed a dream. In his dream the king stood by a river. He saw seven fat cows come up out of the water and eat grass in the meadow nearby. And behold, seven lean cows came up out of the river and ate up the seven fat cows in the meadow.

King Pharaoh awoke, but he could not think what the dream meant. When he went back to sleep, he dreamed again.

In this dream the king saw seven good, full ears of corn come upon one stalk.

And behold, seven thin, sparse ears of corn came upon the stalk and ate up the seven good, full ears of corn.

When Pharaoh awoke in the morning, he was worried. He called all the magicians and wise men of Egypt and told them the dreams. But there was none who could tell the king what they meant.

The chief butler, who heard it all, remembered something. He turned to Pharaoh. "I have just thought of something," he told the king. "When you were angry with me and put me and the chief baker in prison, we, too, had dreams.

"And there was with us in the prison a young man, a Hebrew, a servant to the captain of the guard. He told us what our dreams meant, and it came true just as he said. I was restored to my place as cupbearer, and the chief baker was hanged."

Pharaoh did not wait. "Bring the young Hebrew from prison," he ordered.

Quickly Joseph bathed and dressed himself in fresh clothes, and came before the king.

"I have dreamed a dream," Pharaoh told Joseph, "and no one can tell me what it means. I have heard that you understand all about dreams."

Joseph bowed low before the king. "It is not I who understands," Joseph explained. "My God will give the meaning of Pharaoh's dream."

So the king told Joseph his dream.

"In my dream," Pharaoh began, "I stood by a river. Seven fat cows came up out of the river

and ate grass in the meadow nearby. Then came seven lean cows, worse looking than any I ever saw in Egypt. And behold, the seven lean cows ate up the seven fat cows in the meadow. But they were still as lean as they had been in the beginning.

"In another dream I saw seven good full ears of corn upon one stalk. And behold, seven thin, sparse ears of corn came upon the stalk and ate up the seven good, full ears of corn.

"I told both these dreams to the magicians," Pharaoh ended, "but none of them could tell their meaning."

"God is speaking to Pharaoh in these dreams," Joseph began. "He is telling Pharaoh what will come to pass. The seven fat cows are seven good years, and the seven good ears of corn are seven good years. Both dreams mean the same thing.

"The seven lean cows and the seven bad ears of corn are seven bad years.

"Behold, there shall come seven years of great plenty throughout the land of Egypt. Then there shall come seven years of famine when the great harvests shall be forgotten and the famine shall spread throughout the land.

"This is God's way of helping you get ready

for those years of famine," Joseph explained to the king. "Find a wise man and put him in charge of the land. Let him appoint officers to help him, one for each fifth part of the land of Egypt. Let this man and his officers gather food each of the seven good years and store it away for the seven bad years that will come."

King Pharaoh agreed. "Where shall I find a wiser man than this?" he asked his servants. "A man who is led of the Lord?"

Then the king turned to Joseph. "Since God has given you understanding, there is none so wise as you," Pharaoh said. "You shall be over my house and over all the people. Only on the throne will I be greater than you."

Pharaoh took off his ring and put it on Joseph's finger. He gave Joseph a suit of fine linen and put a gold chain about Joseph's neck. Then the king made a great procession. Next to his own chariot came the chariot of Joseph.

"Bow the knee to Joseph," the king ordered, and he made Joseph ruler over all of Egypt.

A Ruler in Egypt

Joseph was now thirty years old. As ruler in the land of Egypt, he had a fine home. He was given a beautiful wife. He had a new name, the Egyptian name of Zaphnathpaaneah. And he had a new job, the heavy job of going throughout all the land of Egypt and gathering food during the seven years of plenty, so that there would be food in the years of famine.

In every large city Joseph had storehouses built. There, every year for seven years of plenty, he stored grain.

Now in his time of prosperity Joseph did not forget the Lord. When his two little sons were born he named one Manasseh, for, "God hath made me forget all my toil," he said. The other son Joseph named Ephraim, for, he said, "God hath caused me to be fruitful in the land of my affliction."

At last the seven years of plenty in the land of Egypt were ended. Then the seven years of need began, the years when there were no harvests. In all the land of Egypt no grain grew.

Hungry and lean, the people came to King Pharaoh, begging for **bread**. To every one Pharaoh gave the same reply. "Go to Joseph," he said. "Do whatever Joseph says."

And Joseph opened the great storehouses he had built and sold grain to the people of Egypt.

The drought had spread into other countries, and many of them depended upon Egypt for grain. From these countries too came long caravans to carry corn back to their own lands.

Even in the fruitful land of Canaan there was famine, and the people there heard of the grain stored in Egypt.

Old Jacob told his sons about it one day. "I hear that there is corn in Egypt," he said. "Go there and buy grain that we may live and not die."

So Joseph's ten brothers went down to buy corn in Egypt. The youngest brother Benjamin did not go. "Some hurt might come to him," Jacob feared.

And it came about that one day Joseph saw familiar Hebrew faces in the crowd that stood before him to buy grain.

"Where do you come from?" Joseph asked.

"From the land of Canaan, to buy food," replied the sons of Jacob. And Joseph knew his brothers, but the brothers knew him not.

Joseph was remembering something. He was remembering a dream, and some older brothers who laughed at it.

"You are spies," Joseph accused the sons of Jacob. "You have come to see how little harvest there is in Egypt."

"No, no," the brothers argued. "We are all one man's sons, true men and not spies. Once there were twelve brothers. The youngest is with our father back home in Canaan."

"You are spies," Joseph insisted. "One of you

may go home. The rest of you I will keep in prison until he returns with that youngest brother of whom you speak."

Then Joseph had all ten of the brothers put into the prison dungeon.

Perhaps he was thinking of a dark, deep pit into which a seventeen-year-old boy had been thrown years ago. The brothers remembered that long-ago pit, too. They remembered the wrong they had done Joseph, for they said, "We are verily guilty concerning our brother. We saw his hurt and his fear when he begged us not to put him into the pit that day. And we paid no attention to him. This is our punishment for that day."

Joseph understood the Hebrew words they said, though the brothers did not know it. "I will keep one of you bound," Joseph told his brothers. "The rest of you may take corn home to your families."

So Joseph took Simeon and bound him. Then Joseph commanded his servants to fill the sacks of the brothers with corn and to put in with the corn the money each man had paid him. "Give them food for their journey," Joseph commanded his servants, and it was done.

The brothers loaded the sacks of corn on their donkeys and were soon on their way. That night at the inn when it was time to feed the donkeys, one brother found his money in the mouth of the sack. "Look!" he shouted, "my money is here." The brothers looked. Sure enough, there was the money. The brothers were afraid. "What is this that God has done to us?" they questioned as they made their way home.

Back in Canaan old Jacob was waiting to hear all that had happened. "The ruler in Egypt spoke roughly to us and took us for spies," his sons told him. "When we told him of you and of our family, he demanded that Simeon be left with him until we brought our corn home. We are to take Benjamin back with us when we go again unto Egypt. Then the ruler promises to release Simeon."

As they told their story, the sons of Jacob were emptying their sacks. Suddenly they found in their sacks the rest of the money. "Look!" they shouted. "The rest of the money which we took to Egypt to pay for the corn!"

But old Jacob was not interested in money just

then. Sadly he shook his head. "I sorrow for my children," he said. "Joseph is gone, and Simeon is gone, and now you want to take Benjamin away from me."

Reuben spoke first. "I will take care of Benjamin," he promised. "You may keep my own two sons as a sign of my pledge to you."

But Jacob could not be comforted. "Benjamin shall not leave me," he argued. "If he does, there will be yet more sorrow for me."

And for a time nothing more was said about taking Benjamin to Egypt.

In the land of Canaan the famine grew worse. Soon all the food brought from Egypt was gone.

"Go back to Egypt and buy more food," Jacob told his sons.

Judah shook his head. "The ruler solemnly

commanded that we bring Benjamin with us when we returned. We cannot return to Egypt without him."

A long time they argued. "I will take care of Benjamin," Judah promised. "Unless he goes with us, all of us will die for lack of food. I will bring Benjamin safely home again. I give you my word."

At last Jacob was convinced. Even Benjamin could not live without food, he knew. "If it must be, it must be," he told his sons. "Take a gift to the ruler. Take some of our fruits. Take a little balm and a little honey. Take spices and myrrh and nuts and almonds. And take double money to pay back that which you found in your sacks. And take your youngest brother Benjamin. And the Lord God be merciful unto you, that the ruler may send Simeon and Benjamin back with you again."

The sons of Jacob did just as their father said. They took the presents. They took double money in their hands. And they took young Benjamin. Soon they were in the land of Egypt again, standing before Joseph.

Quickly Joseph spoke to a servant. "Take these

men to my home, and prepare a good dinner for them."

The sons of Jacob were afraid as they followed the servant to Joseph's house. They tried to explain to the servant about coming before to buy food and of their finding the money in the grain.

"We have brought enough money to pay for the corn we got last time and this time, too," they said.

"I know about the money," the servant assured them. "It is a gift."

Then the servant brought Simeon to his brothers. Together they entered the house of Joseph. Together they bathed their tired, dusty feet and gave food to their donkeys. Together they made ready the present they had brought for the ruler of Egypt. When he came they offered their gift and bowed low before him.

Politely Joseph asked how they were. "Is your father well?" he questioned. "Your old father about whom you told me last time? Is he yet living?"

"Our father is in good health," the sons of Jacob assured the ruler. And again they bowed low before him.

As he looked at them Joseph had eyes only for Benjamin. "Is this your youngest brother?" Joseph asked.

The brothers bowed.

"God bless you, my son," Joseph said, and he left his brothers.

In his own room, Joseph wept, wept for the long lonely years away from home, wept for his youngest brother who reminded him so much of his mother, wept for the memory of his father's face.

When he returned to his brothers, Joseph ordered that food be set before them. But for Benjamin he ordered five times as much food as for any of the others.

There was a great feast for the sons of Jacob.

A New Family in Goshen

Never in the two years of the famine had the sons of Jacob had such a feast. Before them Joseph had had placed all the good foods of Egypt—the meats, the melons, the vegetables, and the cakes. While they were eating, Joseph was talking to his steward. He had one more test for his brothers.

"Fill the men's sacks with as much food as they can carry," Joseph directed. "Put every man's money in his sack's mouth. And put my silver cup in the sack of the youngest, together with his corn money."

When morning came, the sons of Jacob started home. They had gone only a short way when they heard the clatter of horse's hoofs. Looking back they saw the steward of Joseph.

"Halt!" he was shouting.

The brothers stopped.

"Why have you rendered my master evil for good?" asked the steward.

The brothers listened in amazement.

"My master's silver cup has been stolen," the steward went on. "One of you has taken it."

"Not so," protested the brothers. "We have tried to pay for the corn in our sacks. Certainly we would not steal. If you find the silver cup on any of us, let that one be put to death, and the rest of us will be slaves in the land of Egypt."

Speedily the brothers took down their sacks and opened them, and the silver cup was found in Benjamin's sack.

The brothers wept. Slowly they turned their donkeys about and made their way back to Joseph's house.

"What is this that you have done?" Joseph asked.

Judah spoke for the brothers. "What shall we say?" he began. "How shall we clear ourselves? Behold, we have come back to be your slaves, all of us and he also with whom the cup was found."

Joseph shook his head. "No," he said, "only the man in whose sack the cup was found shall be my servant. Get you to your father."

Judah came nearer. "Oh, my lord," he begged. "Listen, I pray you. Down in the land of Canaan there is an old man, our father. He loves this youngest son of his, loves him more than any of us. He will die if the boy does not return. I gave my promise to bring Benjamin back safely. Now, therefore, I pray you, let me stay here as your servant, and let Benjamin go with his brothers to his father in the land of Canaan."

Joseph had heard enough. "I am Joseph," he cried. "Does my father yet live?"

The brothers stood still. They made no answer.

"Come near to me," Joseph invited.

The brothers stepped nearer.

Joseph went on. "I am Joseph your brother whom you sold into Egypt. But do not worry about that. God sent me here to preserve lives. For two years there have been no harvests. There will be none for five more years. Go quickly to my father and tell him God has made me ruler of all Egypt. Bring my father to this land. He and you and your families shall live near me in the land of Goshen."

So Joseph made himself known to his brothers. He kissed them and the sound of rejoicing was heard even in the house of Pharaoh.

To each of his brothers Joseph gave a new suit of clothes, but to Benjamin he gave three hundred pieces of silver and five new suits of clothes.

To his father Joseph sent wagons to bring him and his possessions to Egypt. He sent ten donkeys loaded with good things from Egypt and ten other donkeys loaded with corn and bread and meat.

Back in the land of Canaan old Jacob waited. One day he saw a cloud of dust. He heard the rumble of wagon wheels. "My sons come!" Jacob cried, and he hastened to see if Benjamin was with them.

What was it that the sons were shouting? Benjamin was shouting it, too.

"Joseph is alive! He is ruler over all the land of Egypt."

The news was too good for Jacob to believe. But when he saw the presents and the wagons which Joseph had sent to carry him to Egypt, when he heard all that had happened, old Jacob was happy indeed. "It is enough," he said. "Joseph my son is yet alive. I will go and see him before I die."

Soon the family of Jacob was on its way. Slowly the caravan moved from the land of Canaan, for there were men and women and children and

cattle and goods. At last they reached Egypt.

News of their arrival reached Joseph. He made ready his chariot and rode to meet his father. At last they were together again.

For a long time old Jacob held his son close. "I can die happy now," he whispered, "for I have seen your face again."

Proudly Joseph presented his father to King Pharaoh. And Jacob blessed Pharaoh. Then Jacob and his sons went out to the land of Goshen to live there with their herds and families in the land which Joseph had provided for them. There Jacob lived for seventeen years.

Before he died, Jacob gave his blessing to the sons of Joseph. And to Joseph he gave a promise, "God shall be with you, and bring your family again into the land of your fathers."

Joseph never forgot that promise. When he was an old man he called his sons to him and passed it on to them.

"I am dying," Joseph said, "but do not be discouraged. God has not forgotten us. Some day he will bring you out of this land of strangers to your own homeland where your father and his fathers lived long ago."

Joseph was quiet for a while. Then he spoke again.

"I will be buried here in Egypt, in the land of strangers. When the time comes that you return to our homeland, take my bones with you. I shall sleep at last in the soil of Canaan."

So Joseph died when he was a hundred and ten years old, and his body was buried in Egypt, in the land of strangers.

But Joseph's sons did not forget. Years later, when Moses led the descendants of Joseph out of Egypt, they carried the bones of Joseph and buried them in the homeland he had loved.

The Deliverer

Years had passed since Joseph brought his father and his brothers and their families to live near him in the land of Goshen. Now Joseph was dead. His brothers were dead. Yet their children and their children's children lived on in Egypt. There were a great many of them. A new king was on the throne, a king who neither knew nor cared about Joseph.

One day the king called his counselors. "These Hebrew people, the children of Israel, are more than we," he said. "Suppose they should arise and fight against us. Let us see to it that they are not so strong."

So the Egyptians made slaves of the children of Israel. They set cruel taskmasters over them. And the children of Israel worked as they had never worked before. Some of them worked in the quarries and some in the brick ovens; some of them worked in the fields and some on the building of great cities for the king.

But still the children of Israel grew in number.

The king was enraged. He gave orders that every boy child born in a Hebrew home should be killed. In all the land of Goshen there was great sorrow.

In one home there was joy and sorrow and fear one day—joy that a little boy had been born, sorrow for the cruel order of the king, and fear that the king's soldier might find the baby and kill him.

For three months the mother hid her baby. But he was growing. His cry grew louder and it was hard to keep people from hearing it.

For a long time the mother thought. Then she took some of the bulrushes that grew by the river and plaited them into a little basket boat. She filled every crack tightly with slime and pitch. When it was dry, she placed her baby

son in it. Then she left the little basket in the grass and rushes at the river's edge. Nearby she left Miriam, the baby's sister, to keep watch.

Step, step, step, Miriam heard light footsteps coming down the path to the river. Peeking through the tall rushes, she saw King Pharaoh's daughter coming to bathe. With the princess were her maids.

The princess saw the little basket boat first. "Look," she called to her maids, "bring that basket to me."

Soon the basket was in the princess's hand. She lifted the lid and saw a beautiful baby boy. The baby blinked his eyes. He began to cry.

"It is one of the Hebrew children," the princess told her maids.

Little Miriam had been watching. Straight to the princess she ran. "Shall I go and call a Hebrew woman to nurse the baby for you?" she asked.

The princess nodded. "Go," she said.

Little Miriam ran fast to find her own dear mother. Soon they were back.

"Take this child and nurse him for me," the princess directed, "and I will pay you wages."

There was a happy time that night in the little house where Miriam and the baby lived with their mother and father and little brother Aaron. Their baby was safe. There were many happy days there, for it was not until he had had several birthdays that the princess took the little boy to the palace to live with her and gave him the name *Moses*. "For," she explained, "I drew him out of the water."

All the time things were getting harder for the Hebrew people. "Send us a deliverer," the people prayed day after day.

God was already answering their prayers, for in the palace of the king, a little boy was growing up. He was being taught all the skill and learning of the Egyptians. His name was Moses.

Little Moses grew bigger. Years passed. At last he was a man. He was interested in all that went on about him. Especially he was interested in the Hebrew people who were slaves in the land of Egypt. One day when he saw a taskmaster mistreating one of the Hebrews, he killed him. Then, because he was afraid of the king, Moses ran away from Egypt to the land of Midian. There he met some beautiful girls watering their

father's sheep. Politely Moses drew water for them. When the sheep were no longer thirsty, the girls led them back home.

"Why are you home so early?" the girls' father asked.

"An Egyptian helped us and drew water for our flocks," the girls explained.

"Bring him home to eat with us," their father directed.

So Moses came to the house of Jethro. Later he married one of Jethro's daughters.

Back in Egypt the Hebrews were having a harder time than ever. Over and over again they made their prayer, "Send us a deliverer, O Lord. Deliver us from the hand of the Egyptians."

They did not know it, but God was already answering their prayer. Out in the pasture land of Midian, a man was learning all there was to know about outdoor life. He was learning to be strong and patient and to trust God more every day. His name was Moses.

One day as Moses watched sheep on a mountain, he saw a bush burning. The strange thing about it was that the bush burned and burned, yet it was not consumed.

"I will stop right here and see why this is," Moses said to himself. He stood still. As he watched, he heard a voice.

"Moses," the voice called, "Moses!"

"Here I am," Moses answered.

"Take off your shoes, Moses," said the voice of God, "for this is holy ground.

"I am the God of your father," the voice went on, "the God of Abraham, the God of Isaac, and the God of Jacob."

Moses bowed his head.

Again God spoke. "I have seen the affliction and hardship of my people who are slaves in the land of Egypt. I have heard their cries as they were beaten. I have seen their sorrows. I am planning to deliver them. I will bring them to a good land flowing with milk and honey.

"Come now, Moses, and I will send you to King Pharaoh that you may bring forth my people out of the land of Egypt."

Moses started in surprise. "Who am I that I should go unto King Pharaoh and bring forth the children of Israel?" he questioned.

"I will be with you," God promised. "As a sign of this, when you have brought them out of Egypt, you shall worship God on this very mountain."

"Suppose the people do not believe me. Suppose they say God did not send me, what then?" Moses wanted to know.

"What is that in your hand?" God asked.

"A rod," Moses answered, "a shepherd's rod."

"Cast it on the ground," God directed. And when Moses cast it on the ground, the rod became a serpent.

"Pick it up by the tail," God directed. And when Moses picked the serpent up by the tail, it was a rod again.

Other signs and wonders the Lord showed unto Moses, but still he hesitated. "I am a poor speaker, Lord," he argued. "I am slow of speech and of slow tongue."

"Who made men's mouths?" the Lord asked. "Go, and I will be with your mouth, and teach you what to say."

Still Moses hesitated.

So God promised him a helper. "Your brother Aaron will help you," God promised. "He can be your spokesman to the people."

Soon Moses was talking to his father-in-law. "Let me return to my people in the land of Egypt," he begged.

Jethro understood. "Go in peace," he said. So Moses and his family started on the long journey back to Egypt.

On the way Aaron met him. Moses told him the words the Lord had spoken and together they went to the elders of the Hebrew people. They, too, believed, and they bowed their heads and thanked God for the deliverer he had sent to them.

At the Court of the Pharaoh

There was much to be done before the Hebrew people could be led out of Egypt. They must learn to trust the deliverer God had sent. They must plan for the long journey. They must learn to manage their own affairs.

One day Moses and Aaron went to the court of Pharaoh. "Thus saith the Lord God of Israel," they told the king, " 'Let my people go into the wilderness and have a service of sacrifice and worship to me.' "

Pharaoh was not interested. "Who is the Lord that I should obey his voice?" he shouted. "Why are you keeping these slaves of mine from their work? Get out of my sight."

When Moses and Aaron were gone, Pharaoh called the taskmasters to him. "Make my Hebrew slaves work harder," he commanded. "Give them no more straw with which to make bricks. Have them gather up their own straw and yet make as many bricks as before. Let there be no more time for talk of sacrifice to their God."

The taskmasters did as Pharaoh commanded. Far and wide the Hebrews went to hunt straw for brickmaking. It took so much time that they could not make as many bricks as they had before. When they were short, the taskmasters ordered them beaten.

Some of the Hebrew overseers protested to Pharaoh. "We have no straw," they explained. "How can we make as many bricks as before?"

But Pharaoh paid no attention to them. "You are idle!" he shouted. "That is why we have this talk of sacrifice to your God. Go to your work. No straw will be given you, and yet you must deliver the full amount of bricks."

As the overseers left the court, they met Moses and Aaron. "You have made matters worse for the Hebrew people," they accused. "Pharaoh will kill all of us."

Moses was puzzled. "Lord," he prayed, "why did you send me to do this job? Since I came to Pharaoh to speak in your name, he has done more evil to the people, and they are not yet delivered."

"I am the Lord," God told Moses. "Speak unto the Israelites and tell them that I will yet bring them out of Egypt unto the land which I have promised them."

But the people were discouraged by their cruel bondage and could not believe the words of Moses.

Again the Lord spoke to Moses. "Go unto Pharaoh," he commanded. "Tell him to let my people go."

"Pharaoh will not listen to me," Moses argued.

Nevertheless, at the word of the Lord, Moses and Aaron again stood before the wicked king. "Unless you let these Hebrew people go out of your land, the Lord will bring great plagues on Egypt," Moses and Aaron warned.

But Pharaoh would not let the people go.

First there came a plague of blood in the River Nile. The fish died, and the Egyptians had no water to drink.

"Unless you let these Hebrew people go out of your land, the Lord will plague Egypt with frogs," Moses warned Pharaoh.

But Pharaoh was stubborn. He would not let the people go.

So the plague of frogs came. There were frogs in the fields and frogs in the houses. There were frogs in the beds and frogs in the cook ovens. There were frogs in the clothes and frogs in the bread bowls.

Pharaoh was afraid. "I will let the Hebrew people go," he promised. "Get rid of the frogs and I will do as you say."

So Moses prayed unto God, and the frogs died.

But Pharaoh did not keep his promise.

Then came the plague of lice when all men and beasts were covered with crawling vermin.

Still Pharaoh protested that the Hebrews must remain in Egypt.

"There will come a plague of flies on all the Egyptians," Moses warned. And it was so. Swarms of flies came upon the houses and the people and the servants of the Egyptians, but in the land of Goshen where the Hebrew slaves lived, there was no plague of flies.

"I will let the Hebrews go," Pharaoh promised again. "Pray your God that the plague of flies be removed." And it was so.

But again Pharaoh was stubborn. He would not let the Hebrews go.

"There will be a plague of disease among all the cattle of the Egyptians," Moses warned. And it was so. Upon all the cattle of the Egyptians, upon their horses, their donkeys, their camels, their oxen, and their sheep, a plague of disease came. All over the land the cattle died, but in the land of Goshen there was no plague upon the cattle of the Hebrew people.

But Pharaoh did not let the people go.

Then came the plague of boils—boils on men and on beasts, boils so terrible that some have called them the black leprosy.

But still Pharaoh did not let the people go.

Again Moses warned Pharaoh. "Unless you let the Hebrew people go," he declared, "there shall come a plague of hail such as the land of Egypt has never seen." And it was so.

There came thunder and hail and fire. And the hail smote all in the fields of the Egyptians— men, beasts, grass, and trees.

Only in the land of Goshen, where the children of Israel were, was there no hail.

Pharaoh sent for Moses. "Pray unto your God that the plague cease," he begged. "Then I will let the children of Israel go."

So Moses prayed unto the Lord, and the plague ceased.

But Pharaoh did not keep his promise. He did not let the children of Israel go.

"There shall come a plague of locusts," the Lord warned Pharaoh through Moses.

So the locusts came in great swarms. They covered the earth. They ate the vegetables that had escaped the hailstorm. They filled the houses and fields of the Egyptians. Throughout all the land there was not a green thing left.

Even Pharaoh's servants protested this time. "Let the Hebrew people go," they begged, "else Egypt may be destroyed."

So Pharaoh agreed. Still he did not keep his promise.

There came a plague of darkness, a thick darkness which lasted for three days, *but all the children of Israel had light in their dwellings.*

Still Pharaoh would not let the children of Israel go. "Get out of my sight," he ordered Moses. "If you come again into my presence, I will kill you."

So Moses went out from the presence of Pharaoh to talk with the Lord.

"One more plague I will bring," the Lord declared. "Get the children of Israel ready to leave. For at midnight the oldest child in every Egyptian home shall die. And there shall be great sorrow throughout all Egypt."

So Moses prepared the children of Israel to go out of the land of Egypt. They ate together the Passover supper. On the door of every home in Goshen there was the blood of the Passover lamb that the death angel might pass over that house.

So it was that at midnight the firstborn in every home, from the firstborn of Pharaoh to the firstborn of all his servants and all the cattle died. And there was a great cry throughout all Egypt.

Pharaoh sent for Moses and Aaron. "Get out of my land," he begged, "you and all the children of Israel, with your flocks and possessions."

So it was that the children of Israel went forth out of Egypt.

Four hundred and thirty years before, Joseph had brought his father and his brothers down to live in the land of Goshen. Now their children's children were leaving Egypt for a new land. In spite of their hurry and danger, these Hebrews did not forget Joseph. With them they carried his bones just as he had directed.

And the Lord went before them by day in a pillar of cloud, to lead them the way; and by night in a pillar of fire, to give them light.

In this way he led them to camp by the Red Sea.

Journey to a New Land

The children of Israel were encamped by the Red Sea. Before them lay its deep waters. Behind them lay Egypt. Behind them on the road from Egypt came Pharaoh's chariots and armies to capture the children of Israel and take them again to be slaves. The children of Israel heard the rumble of Pharaoh's chariots drawing near.

"Why did you bring us out of Egypt?" the people questioned Moses. "It would have been better to serve the Egyptians than to die here."

"Fear not," Moses assured them. "The Lord shall fight for you." And Moses prayed unto God.

At once God answered Moses. "Speak unto the children of Israel and tell them to go forward," God commanded.

Forward! Forward was into the waters of the Red Sea.

"Stretch out your rod over the Red Sea," God directed Moses, "and the children of Israel shall walk over on dry land."

Nearer came the chariots of the Egyptians. Between them and the children of Israel was the pillar which lighted the Israelites like glowing fire but was a cloud turned toward the Egyptians.

Moses stretched out his rod over the sea.

And the Lord caused the sea to go back by a strong east wind all that night, and made the sea dry land, and the waters were divided. And the children of Israel went into the midst of the sea upon the dry ground: and the waters were a wall unto them on their right and on their left.

The last Israelite was over. The Egyptians tried to follow, but their chariot wheels sank in the damp sand.

"Stretch out your rod again," God commanded Moses, "that the waters may come upon the Egyptians."

Moses stretched forth his hand over the sea, and the waters came together again, and covered the chariots and the horsemen and all the hosts of Pharaoh so that not so much as one of them remained.

Thus the Lord saved Israel that day out of the hand of the Egyptains . . . and the people believed the Lord, and his servant Moses.

On into the wilderness Moses led the children

of Israel. When they were thirsty and there was only bitter water to drink, Moses prayed unto the Lord and the Lord showed him a tree, which he cast into the waters and the waters were made sweet.

When the people were hungry and there was no food, Moses prayed unto the Lord, and the Lord sent manna, small as hoar frost and sweet as honey.

All this time God, through Moses, was teaching the people how to live happily together, how to worship and serve the only true God.

It was at Mount Sinai that God gave Moses ten great laws written on tablets of stone, the laws which are called the Ten Commandments. He also gave laws about little things. One law reminded the people not to bother a bird on her nest. One reminded them to pay every man his wages when they were due. There were laws about health and laws about good foods to eat, laws about taking care of cattle and about treating neighbors right.

Now the people needed a special place to worship God. So God gave Moses a plan for building a great tent house where the people might come and worship. They gathered together beautiful things— gold and silver and brass, fine linen and silk of blue and purple and scarlet, and rams' and badgers' skins dyed a beautiful red. The people brought oil for the lights and spices for  sweet-smelling incense. They brought onyx and other precious stones. They brought smooth wood for tables and brass for great curtain holders. It was a beautiful tabernacle that the people built as a place to worship the Lord, and God made a promise concerning it.

"There," he said, "I will meet with the children of Israel, and the place shall be beautiful with my glory. And I will dwell among the children of Israel, and they shall know that I am the Lord their God, that brought them forth out of the land of Egypt."

At last the work was finished. Then a cloud covered the great tent house, and the glory of the Lord filled it.

When the cloud lifted up from over the tabernacle, the children of Israel went onward in their journey. But if the cloud were not taken up, they waited.

For the cloud of the Lord was upon the tabernacle by day, and fire was on it by night.

Sometimes the people complained. Sometimes they sinned greatly. Then Moses would pray for them, and somehow, the Lord would guide them in the right things to do.

At last they came near the borders of the land of promise. There Moses sent twelve men to spy out the land and see what it was like, what kind of people lived there, what the fruits and crops were, whether the cities were walled and whether the people lived in tents or in houses of wood.

It was the time of the first ripe grapes when the spies went out. After forty days they came back. With them they brought a great cluster of grapes. "It is a good land that we have seen," the spies agreed, "a land full of milk and honey." But there the agreement stopped.

"The people of the land are great, and strong like giants," ten of the spies said. "We look like grasshoppers compared to them. We could never take their land."

But Caleb and Joshua had another report. "Let us go up at once and possess the land," they said, "for we are well able to overcome it."

The children of Israel believed the report of the ten spies. They murmured against Moses and Aaron. "We wish we had died in Egypt or in the wilderness," they wailed. "Let us return to Egypt."

"The Lord is with us. Do not be afraid," Caleb and Joshua counseled. But still the people complained. They would not go on.

Just as he always did, Moses prayed unto the Lord. "Forgive the people," Moses prayed. "Forgive their lack of trust in Thee."

And the Lord did forgive the people. But because they would not trust him to help them win the land, they wandered in the wilderness for forty years. And when the time came to enter the land of promise, no one who had been over twenty years old when the spies made their report was left to go in.

Miriam had died. Aaron had died. And Moses was growing old. One day Moses made a great speech to the people. He reminded them of how God had led them safely out of the land of Egypt, how God had cared for them, how God was leading them to a promised land. He gave the people his blessing. Then Moses went up from the plains of Moab into the mountain of Nebo. Not so far away God showed him the land of Gilead and the city of Jericho. "This is the land which I promised Abraham and his children long ago," God said. "This is the land of promise to which I have been leading the children of Israel."

And there, as he was looking at that beautiful land, Moses died. The Lord buried him in a valley of Moab, and no man knows the place of his grave.

God called Joshua, the son of Nun, to be the new leader of the children of Israel. Now it was through him that God led his people. And God brought them unto the land of Canaan just as he had promised.

David of Bethlehem

In the fields outside Bethlehem the boy David kept watch over his father's sheep. On pleasant days he led them to green pastures to eat the grass. When they were thirsty, he led them to drink the clear waters of the brook that ran through the meadow. When the sheep were hurt, David poured oil on their sores. When the way led through rough, dangerous places, David used his crook to keep the sheep from falling.

One day a lion slipped up on the flock of sheep and stole away a lamb. Before he could hurt the lamb David was after him. He struck the lion and seized the lamb from its mouth. Then he killed the lion and carried the frightened lamb safely home on his shoulder. Another day a bear carried off a lamb, but David rescued this one, too, and brought it safely home to the fold.

There was another thing David did as he watched over his sheep. He made soft music on his harp. When the birds sang, David listened. Then he ran his fingers over the strings of his harp, and the harp sang too. When the waters of the brook sang as they tumbled down the hill, David listened. Then he ran his fingers over the strings of his harp, and the harp sang with music like a running stream. When the wind blew, David listened. Then he ran his fingers over the strings of his harp, and the harp sang music like the sound of breezes in the trees. David thought of God, and his fingers on the strings of his harp made music to praise God for his care. Sometimes David sang as he played on his harp. "The Lord is my shepherd," David sang.

One day as David watched the sheep, a servant came running to him. "Come into the town," the servant panted. "Your father wants you at once. The prophet Samuel is there, and strange things are going on."

"What things?" David wanted to know.

The servant shook his head.

"I do not know," he said, "but one by one your seven older brothers have been taken before the prophet. Each time the prophet has shaken his head and said, 'The Lord hath not chosen this one.' When all seven had passed by, the prophet asked, 'Are these all your children?'

"Your father smiled at that, Master David. 'All except the youngest,' he answered. And the prophet ordered him to send for you."

As they talked, they had been on their way to the village. Now they were there, and young David stood before Samuel, the prophet. A good-looking boy he was, red-cheeked, and tall.

Samuel looked at the boy. Then he heard a voice. "Arise," said the Lord, "anoint him, for this is the one."

And Samuel took the horn of oil he carried with him and anointed David.

Perhaps neither David nor his family knew exactly what the anointing meant, for Samuel went back to his home in Remah, and young David went back to the fields outside Bethlehem to tend his father's sheep.

One day a messenger came to the house of Jesse, David's father. "King Saul is sick and troubled," the messenger said. "Send your shepherd son, David, to play sweet music for him."

Of course Jesse was glad for his son to play for the king. He gave David a donkey, a bottle of wine, some bread, and some meat, to take as a gift to King Saul.

The minute King Saul saw David he liked him. When Saul was feeling ill, David would run his fingers over the strings of his harp, and play again the music of the birds and the brook and the trees. He would sing to King Saul, too. Perhaps he sang, "The Lord is my shepherd."

David came to be Saul's armor bearer. For a while he lived in the palace. And for a time Saul was well of sickness when he listened to the music of David. Then David went back to his father's fields to care for the sheep.

Now the Philistines and the people of David's country were at war. The Philistines were a mighty people. Their army lined up on a mountain on one side of the valley. On the other side of the valley were the armies of Israel.

One day there came out from the armies of the

Philistines a champion named Goliath. He was a giant, more than eleven feet tall. He had a helmet of brass on his head, and he was clothed in heavy brass armor. He had a brass coat and a brass breastplate, and brass leggings. He had a mighty iron spear, and the staff of the spear was like a weaver's beam. Before the giant went his armor bearer.

Tall and fierce, Goliath stood on the hill and called unto the armies of Israel.

"Why bring out your armies?" he taunted. "I am a Philistine. Choose a man of the Israelites to fight me. If he wins, we, the Philistines, will be your slaves. If I win, you, the Israelites, shall become our servants."

Day after day Goliath made the same challenge. But not a man of the armies of the Israelites dared fight him.

David had three brothers in the army. One night David's father announced that his son must go on a trip. "You must take food to your brothers in the army," Jesse told David. "Take a measure of parched corn and ten loaves of bread to their camp. Carry ten cheeses to the captain. Keep your ears open and bring me news of your brothers."

Next morning David rose up early. He left his sheep with a keeper. Then he set out for the camp of Israel where he was soon giving the food to his brothers and hearing all about the battle. He heard all about Goliath, too. "Who is this giant to defy the armies of God?" David asked. "Will no one go out to meet him?"

When Saul heard of David's question, he sent for him.

David was ready. "Let not the people be a-fraid," David told Saul. "I will go and fight with this giant Philistine."

"You cannot do that," Saul argued. "You are but a boy."

"I am strong," David assured the king. "One day when I was keeping my father's sheep, there came a lion and a bear and took a lamb out of the flock. I went after them and rescued the lamb. And I killed both the bear and the lion. The Lord delivered me out of the paw of the lion and out of the paw of the bear, and he will deliver me out of the hand of this Philistine."

King Saul nodded. "Go," he said, "and the Lord be with you."

But before he sent David away, the king had him put on a suit of royal armor, with a helmet of brass upon his head, and a heavy coat of brass around his shoulders.

David picked up the heavy sword which the king had given him, but somehow he felt cramped and awkward. "I am not used to these," he told Saul. "I cannot fight this way."

Slowly David took off the armor which the king had given him. He laid aside the great sword. In place of them he took his shepherd staff and his sling. He chose five smooth stones from the brook in the meadow and put them in his shepherd's bag. Then he set out for the camp of the Philistines. For the fortieth time now Goliath

had shouted his challenge. But no man had come to fight him. Now someone was coming, but it was a boy, not a man.

Goliath was angry when he saw David. "Am I a dog," he roared, "that you come to fight me with a staff?" And Goliath cursed David by all the heathen gods of the Philistines.

Steadily David went on. "You fight with a spear and a sword and a shield," he told Goliath, "but I come in the name of the Lord God of the armies of Israel. This day will the Lord deliver you into my hand. And all the people shall know that the Lord saveth not with sword and spear: for the battle is the Lord's and he will give you into our hands."

On went David.

Nearer came Goliath.

Faster ran David. As he ran, he put his hand in his bag and took out a stone and put it in his sling. Then he let go the shot.

Straight to its mark went the stone from David's sling. It hit the Philistine in his forehead, and the giant fell upon his face to the ground.

David ran forward. Quickly he seized Goliath's sword and cut off the head of the giant.

When the Philistines saw that their champion was dead, they fled.

And King Saul took young David to live in the palace with him.

A Kingly Friend

For a time David enjoyed living in the palace with King Saul. There were good things to eat, and there were servants to wait on him. Best of all, there was Prince Jonathan. Prince Jonathan was King Saul's son, not much older than David.

The two boys had loved each other from the moment they met. Jonathan had taken off his fine coat and belt and given them to David. He had given David his sword and his bow. The two boys worked and played together. Jonathan told David of his life in the court, and David told Jonathan of his life in the fields, of the sheep and of the bears and lions that came sometimes. He played his harp for Jonathan, and the two were together most of the time.

Other people liked David, too. They sang his praises, and Saul became jealous. So jealous he was, that he gave orders to Jonathan and his servants that David be killed.

Perhaps one of the servants would have succeeded, but Jonathan warned David and helped him to get away. One day Jonathan went to his father. "Let not the king sin against David," he begged. "All that he has done is good. Do not kill him."

For a time the king listened to Jonathan. Again he sent for David, but he was still jealous, and one day as David played on his harp, Saul threw his javelin and tried to kill him.

David slipped away, but he knew it would not be safe for him to stay at his father's house. He went to his old friend, the prophet Samuel. And again Jonathan sought to persuade King Saul to treat David kindly.

King Saul was very angry. "Do you not know that you will never be king as long as David lives?" he shouted at Jonathan.

But still Jonathan loved David. One day the two boys made a promise. They promised that they would always love each other and be kind to each other. "And not to me only," Jonathan begged, "but also thou shalt not cut off thy kindness from my house forever: no, not when the Lord hath cut off the enemies of David every one from the face of the earth."

And so David promised.

"I shall speak to my father again," Jonathan said. "Perhaps he will relent and not try to harm you."

"How shall I know what he says?" David asked.

Jonathan thought a moment. "I will go out in the field to shoot arrows," he said. "I will take with me a boy to pick up the arrows. When I shoot an arrow I will send him to find it. If I say, 'The arrows are on this side of thee,' you may know that my father Saul is at peace with you. If I say, 'The arrows are beyond thee,' you must go away at once. Hide in the field and wait."

So David waited. Sure enough, Jonathan came just as he had promised. David could hear the ping of the string on Jonathan's bow. Then he heard Jonathan's call to the boy who carried the arrows, "Is not the arrow beyond thee?" Thus David knew that King Saul was still seeking to hurt him.

When the boy had gone away, David came to say good-by to Jonathan. They wept and kissed each other, and Jonathan said, "Go in peace, for we have both promised in the name of the Lord, saying, 'The Lord be between me and thee, and between my seed and thy seed forever.' "

So David went away, and Jonathan went back
to his father's house.

It was not long before David and Saul met
again. David and his guerrilla band had been
fighting the Philistines, when Saul heard that
he was at Engedi. Saul took three thousand men
and came to kill David. That night the king slept
in the cave of Engedi. His men must have slept,
too, for in the darkness David came to the cave.
A long time he stood and looked at his enemy.
Then he reached down and cut off a piece of
Saul's robe and went away.

Next morning David shouted his greeting to Saul across the valley. "See this piece of your robe," he called. "I could have taken your life last night, but the king is anointed of the Lord. The Lord judge me, for I have never tried to harm you."

At last Saul was convinced. "You are more righteous than I," he said, "for thou hast rewarded me good, whereas I have rewarded thee evil. I know that you will be a king soon. Be good to my family when you come to the throne."

And David promised Saul just as he had once promised Jonathan.

King Saul was right. It was not long until David was king in the land of Israel. There were wars, but David led his armies to victory. And at last the land had peace.

Busy as he was, King David did not forget his promise. Jonathan was dead, and David sorrowed for him. But he did more than sorrow. "Is there yet any that is left of the house of Saul?" he asked one day. "I want to show kindness to him for Jonathan's sake."

"Saul's servant, Ziba, is here," someone told David. "He will know."

David sent for Ziba.

"Is there any of the house of Saul left?" David inquired. "I want to show the kindness of God unto him."

Ziba bowed his head. "Jonathan has a son living," he said, "a son who is lame on both his feet."

"Where is he?" King David asked.

"He is living now in Lodebar, in the house of Machir," Ziba said.

So David sent for Jonathan's son.

Soon the boy was kneeling before the king.

"Mephibosheth," David said gently.

Mephibosheth did not look up. "I am your servant," he whispered.

David reached out his hand. "Fear not," he told Mephibosheth. "I will surely show thee kind-

ness for Jonathan, thy father's sake. I will give you all the lands that were Saul's, and you shall eat at my table every day."

Then King David called Ziba. "I have given unto Mephibosheth all the lands and possessions of Saul," David said. "Get together your sons and servants and farm the land for him. Take care of the fruits and harvest for him. But Mephibosheth shall eat bread at my table just as the king's sons do."

And so it was that David kept the promise he had made years ago to his friend Jonathan.

And Jonathan's lame son, Mephibosheth, ate every day at the king's table.

Four Captive Boys

In the capital city of Babylon, there was great excitement. King Nebuchadnezzar had just returned from capturing the city of Jerusalem in Judah. Nebuchadnezzar had brought back with him the conquered king of Judah. He had brought back captives—men, women, and children. He had even brought back some of the golden vessels from the Temple in Jerusalem. But the captives were the greatest treasures the king had brought, for he needed bright young men in Babylon.

One day the king sent for Ashpenaz, master of his servants. "Look over the captives from Judah," he said. "Find me some smart boys to train here in the palace. Get some young princes if you can, handsome boys, who have made good in the schools of their own land, healthy boys who can grow up into strong men. We will teach these boys all the learning of Babylon, the language and all our ways."

The king set aside a portion of his own food for these boys, and a portion of his wine. Those chosen were to be especially trained for three years.

Now among the boys that Ashpenaz chose were four friends—Daniel, Hananiah, Mishael, and Azariah. The first thing that Ashpenaz did was to give these boys Babylonian names. To Daniel he gave the name of Belteshazzar; to Hananiah the name of Shadrach; to Mishael the name of Meshach; and to Azariah, the name of Abednego. These four Ashpenaz brought to the table to eat of the king's meat and to drink of the king's wine.

Now at home, back in the land of Judah, Daniel's mother had taught him right foods to eat. She had taught him not to eat meat such as the

Babylonians used and that wine gave no strength to body or mind. And *Daniel purposed in his heart that he would not defile himself with the portion of the king's meat, nor with the wine which he drank.* For Daniel had made up his mind to be strong in body and mind.

Politely Daniel asked to be excused from eating the king's food.

Now Melzar, the king's steward, liked Daniel very much, but he shook his head at Daniel's request. "I fear the king," Melzar explained. "He has chosen your meat and drink. When he sees you looking not as well as the other captives, he may cut off my head."

"Let's try something," Daniel begged Melzar. "Let Hananiah, Mishael, Azariah, and myself have cereal to eat and water to drink for ten days. Then compare us with the boys who eat of the king's meat and drink of the king's wine, and see which looks better."

Melzar agreed. Every day for ten days Daniel and his three good friends had cereal to eat and water to drink. Every day for ten days the other boys ate of the king's meat and drank of the king's wine. Then came the test.

And Melzar found Daniel and Hananiah, and Mishael, and Azariah fairer and fatter than all the boys who did eat of the king's meat and drink of the king's wine. So Melzar took away the meat and wine, and Daniel and his three friends continued to eat the right foods just as they had been taught back in their homes in Judah.

Every day God was helping these four wise boys to grow. He gave them knowledge and skill and helped them to learn well. And Daniel had understanding of visions and dreams.

Three years passed, and it was time for King Nebuchadnezzar to look over the boys who had been trained. Ashpenaz brought them before him. And the king found none like Daniel, Hananiah, Mishael, and Azariah. *And in all matters*

*of wisdom and understanding, that the king
enquired of them, he found them ten times better
than all the magicians and astrologers that were
in his realm.*

It was not long until Daniel had an opportunity to use some of the wisdom God had given him. Nebuchadnezzar had been having bad dreams. He could not sleep well, but in the morning when he wanted to tell his dreams, he could not remember them. The wise men of the court could not help him, for they did not know the dreams.

King Nebuchadnezzar was in a rage. "Kill all

the wise men in Babylon," he commanded. And the captain of the king's guard went to carry out his orders.

Now among the wise men of Babylon was Daniel. "Why is the king so hasty?" Daniel asked the captain of the guard. "He has not tried all the wise men."

And Daniel himself went before the king and asked that he be given a little time to think about the bad dreams.

Straight home Daniel went to Hananiah, Mishael, and Azariah. "Let us seek the help of the Lord in understanding this thing," Daniel begged them. And the four friends prayed earnestly.

That night God revealed to Daniel the secret of the king's dream. And Daniel thanked the Lord God for his goodness. This was his prayer:

Blessed be the name of God forever and ever:
For wisdom and might are his:
And he changeth the times and the seasons:

He removeth kings, and setteth up kings:
He giveth wisdom unto the wise...
I thank thee, and praise thee, O thou God of
* my fathers,*
Who hast given me wisdom and might,
And hast made known unto me now what we
* desired of thee:*
For thou hast now made known unto us the
* king's matter.*

Next morning Daniel went before the king.
"Are you able to make known unto me my
dream and its meaning?" the king asked.

Daniel bowed his head. "No wise man or as-
trologer or magician can make known the king's
secret," he said, "but there is a God in heaven
that reveals secrets. This God has revealed to
me the secret of the king's dream."

So Daniel told the king's dream of a great
image crushed by a stone. And Daniel told the
king the meaning of the dream, that one day

the kingdom of God would destroy all the kingdoms of men, and that the kingdom of God should stand forever.

King Nebuchadnezzar fell on his face before Daniel. "Truly," the king said, "your God is a God of gods, and a Lord of kings, and a revealer of secrets."

Then the king gave Daniel fine gifts and made him ruler over the whole province of Babylon and chief of the governors over all the wise men of Babylon.

Even in this high position, Daniel did not forget his friends. At his request the king gave fine jobs to Hananiah whom he called Shadrach, to Mishael whom he called Meshach, and to Azariah whom he called Abednego.

And to Daniel the king gave the best place of all in his own palace.

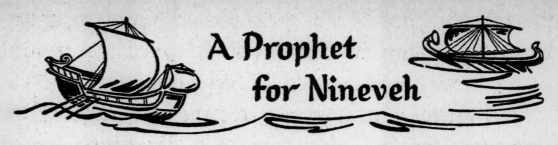

A Prophet for Nineveh

Long ago there was a prophet of God whose name was Jonah. The word of the Lord came unto Jonah one day, saying, "Arise, and go to Nineveh, that great city, cry against it; for their wickedness is come up before me."

Now Jonah was a Jew, and he did not want to go to the city of Nineveh. He did not like the people of Nineveh. He did not like Assyria, in which country was the city of Nineveh. Nineveh was a city unfriendly to the Jews. The people of Nineveh were a people unfriendly to the Jews. The country of Assyria was a country unfriendly to the Jews. Jonah understood that God wanted him to warn Nineveh about its wickedness, so that its people would turn from their wicked ways and be saved from terrible destruction. But Jonah was not interested in helping Nineveh.

As quickly as he could Jonah went down to the seaport city of Joppa and found a ship, going —not to Nineveh but to Tarshish. Jonah paid his fare and got on board. He would not have to preach to those terrible people of Nineveh if he were far away in Tarshish. So Jonah hurried away from the presence of the Lord.

The vessel was loaded and ready to leave. The wind caught the sails and soon the light little ship was out of sight of land.

Then the Lord sent a great wind into the sea, and there was a mighty storm. It seemed that the ship would be broken in pieces. Even the sailors were afraid. They threw overboard all the cargo they could to lighten the ship's load. They cried aloud, and every man prayed unto his god. Still the storm continued.

Now all the while Jonah was fast asleep in the hold of the ship.

At last the shipmaster found him. "Why are you sleeping when all of us are in danger?" the shipmaster asked. "Get up and pray to your God. Perhaps he will help us."

The sailors had another idea. "Come," they said, "let us cast lots, that we may know which one of us is the cause of this storm." So they cast lots, and the lot fell upon Jonah.

The sailors crowded around Jonah. "Tell us," they demanded, "why has this evil storm come upon us? What is your occupation? Where do you come from? What is your country? Of what people do you come?"

So Jonah told the sailors that he was trying to run away from God. "I am a Hebrew," Jonah said. "I fear the Lord, the God of heaven, which hath made the sea and the dry land."

The sailors were more frightened than before. "What must we do?" they asked Jonah. "What must we do that the sea may become calm again?"

Slowly Jonah spoke. "Take me up and cast me into the sea. Then will the sea be calm again, for I know that this storm has come for my sake."

The sailors shook their heads at first. They tried to row the ship to land, but the waves rolled higher and higher. The wind blew fiercer and fiercer.

Then the sailors took Jonah, and threw him into the sea, and immediately the waters were calm.

Jonah did not drown, as the sailors had thought he would, for the Lord had prepared a great fish to swallow up Jonah. And Jonah was inside the great fish three days and three nights.

In those three days and three nights Jonah had time to do some thinking. He did some praying, too. He thanked God for saving him from drowning in the sea. He promised the Lord to obey him always. And at the end of three days the great fish cast Jonah out on dry land.

Then again Jonah heard the voice of the Lord. "Arise," said the Lord, "go unto Nineveh, the great city, and preach unto it the preaching that I bid thee."

So Jonah arose, and this time he went in the right direction. Straight to Nineveh he went to preach as the Lord should direct him.

It was a three days' journey and Jonah was tired when he reached Nineveh. But he did not wait. Immediately he began to preach and warn the people of the destruction that their wickedness was bringing on their city. Even the king of Nineveh listened. "Let every man turn from his evil way and pray unto God," Jonah preached.

And the people listened to Jonah's words. They turned from their wicked ways and prayed unto the Lord. And the Lord forgave them, and saved their city from destruction.

"I knew this would happen," Jonah said. "I knew Nineveh would not be destroyed. The Lord is slow to anger and of great kindness."

And Jonah was right. He had learned at last the thing that God told Moses when he gave him the Ten Commandments, "The Lord is merciful and gracious, long-suffering, and abundant in goodness and truth."

The Promise

In this book you have read many stories from the Old Testament. They are stories of men and women who were sometimes good, sometimes bad. They are stories of men and women who were sometimes afraid, sometimes brave, sometimes sad, sometimes happy. They are stories of men and women who learned that God's laws always work, of men and women who were learning to know God and the help that always comes when people trust him.

But the Old Testament is more than that. It is the story of God: God loving people and seeking to help them, God showing people how to live bravely and happily, God forgiving people when they have been bad, and seeking always to help them to do right things.

And the Old Testament, from which these stories are taken, is more than the story of God's seeking love. For the Old Testament is a promise.

Hinted in the book of Genesis, singing in the words of the Psalms, this promise finds its clear

statement in the prophets. It is the promise of a Saviour who would come some day to show the love of God and bring strength and healing to all who turn to him.

Micah, the prophet, knew about the promise, and, long before its fulfillment, wrote down the place it should come to pass, *But thou, Bethlehem, though thou be little, out of thee shall come the ruler of Israel.*

Isaiah, the prophet, knew about the promise. Looking down the long years to the One who should come, he wrote:

*The people that walked in darkness have seen
   a great light:
They that dwell in the land of the shadow of
   death,
Upon them hath the light shined. . . .
For unto us a child is born, unto us a son is
   given:
And the government shall be upon his
   shoulders:
And his name shall be called
   Wonderful,
   Counsellor,
   The mighty God,
   The everlasting Father,
   The Prince of Peace.*

The coming of Jesus is the promise of the Old
Testament.

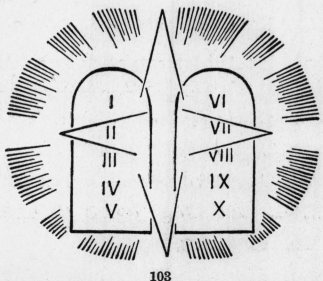

The First Christmas

Once upon a time—the story begins—once upon a time in the little town of Nazareth, in the country of Galilee, in the land of Palestine. It was long ago that this story begins, almost two thousand years ago.

One day the angel of the Lord was sent with glad news to Mary of Nazareth.

"God is pleased with you, Mary," the angel said. "God is going to send you a baby boy. You are going to call his name Jesus, for he will be God's own Son."

Mary was so happy that she had to tell someone the glad news. Far up into the hill country she ran to her cousin Elisabeth.

"God is going to send his own Son to be my baby boy," Mary told Elisabeth. And Mary sang a happy song to thank God for the baby He would send. Mary sang;

"I praise the Lord!
For he is good.
The Lord does great things.
His name is holy."

Back in Nazareth God sent the glad news to good carpenter Joseph.

"God is sending his own Son to be Mary's baby," the angel of the Lord told Joseph one night as he was sleeping. "Take Mary and care for her. And name the baby Jesus, for he shall save his people from their sins."

And so it was that when Mary came back to Nazareth, Joseph took her for his wife. He loved her and cared for her.

In those days Caesar Augustus was the king. One day he sent out a command that every one in the country should be taxed. All the people went to the towns in which they had been born to have their names written in the king's tax book. Mary and Joseph went, too, from the city of Nazareth in Galilee, to the little town of

Bethlehem in Judea, for that was the king's order.

Little Bethlehem was full of people. There was no room for Mary and Joseph in the inn, so they slept that night in a stable. And there, in the quiet dark, while the friendly animals were sleeping and the golden stars shone in the sky, God sent his Son to be Mary's Baby boy. Mary wrapped him in soft clothes. Then she made a bed of straw and laid her Baby in the manger.

In the fields outside little Bethlehem, shepherds were keeping watch over their sheep.

As the shepherds looked up at the sky, they saw a great light shining. They were afraid and hid their faces.

Then they heard the voice of the angel of the Lord.

"Do not be afraid," the angel of the Lord told the shepherds. "I bring you good news. It is happy, happy news, and it is for all people. For you there is born tonight in the little town of Bethlehem, a Saviour. His name is Jesus.

"And this is the way you shall know the Child. You shall find him wrapped in soft baby clothes, lying in a manger-bed."

And suddenly there were with the angel of the Lord many other angels. And all of them together were praising God and singing:

"Glory to God,
In the heavens above.
And on earth—
Peace.
God sends his love
To all people."

As soon as the song was finished, the angels went away into heaven. It was very quiet.

Then a shepherd spoke. "Let us go to little Bethlehem," he said. "Let us find the Child, for the Lord has sent us good news of him."

The other shepherds nodded.

Step, step, step, they started down the road. Then faster and faster they walked until they came at last to little Bethlehem.

And there they found Mary and Joseph, and the Baby Jesus lying in a manger-bed. And the shepherds knelt down and worshiped him.

The news of the Baby Jesus was too wonderful to keep. The shepherds told everyone they met about the Saviour of the world.

"We have seen the Baby Jesus," the shepherds said. "He is lying in a manger-bed in the little town of Bethlehem, just as the angel of the Lord said."

The people wondered at this story of the angel in the shining light, and his message to them. Mary thought about what the shepherds told, and remembered every word.

The shepherds went back to their fields, and as they went, they praised God for all the things they had heard and seen.

Mary and Joseph loved the little Baby God had sent. They named him Jesus just as the angel had told them to do.

And that was the first Christmas.

Little Jesus

Little Baby Jesus snuggled close in his mother's arms. He was forty days old, and Mary and Joseph were carrying him to the big Temple in the city of Jerusalem. They were taking two young pigeons as love gifts to say thank you to God for Baby Jesus.

Mary rode a little donkey and Joseph walked by her side. Down the long road they went, singing sometimes, for they were very happy.

In Jerusalem they left the donkey in a safe place and went to the Temple. Up, up, up the smooth steps they carried the Baby. Inside the shining door Mary and Joseph met old Simeon who had loved God for a long time. Simeon held out his hands and took the Baby in his arms. He hugged him close and loved him. Then Simeon bowed his head. Simeon prayed:

"Thank you, God,
Thank you for letting me see this Baby
Who is to be the Saviour."

Simeon spoke to Mary. "Your child shall be

great," he told her. "He will help many people."

An old woman was in the Temple. Her name was Anna. She, too, had loved God for a long time. Anna loved the little Baby Jesus. She thanked God for him and told everyone the glad news of the Baby who had come to be the Saviour.

Mary and Joseph praised God, too. When the Temple service was over, they carried little Jesus back home to Bethlehem. There the Baby grew and grew. Soon he could walk and run about the little white house. Then he could talk.

One day there came wise men from far away to the big city of Jerusalem. Pad, pad, pad, went

the camels' feet on the streets of the city. Tinkle, tinkle, tinkle, went the silver bells that hung from the camels' necks.

The wise men stopped their camels. They asked a question.

"Where is the Baby who is born to be King of God's people?" the wise men asked. "We have seen his shining star in the sky and have come to praise him."

But no one knew where the Baby was. Even the king did not know.

King Herod called the preachers and writers to come and help him. "Where is the Baby who is born to be king of God's people?" big King Herod asked. He was afraid this Baby might take his place as king some day.

"He is in the little town of Bethlehem," the preachers and writers said. "For so it is written in God's Book:

" 'From out the little town of Bethlehem shall come the Baby who is to be
king of God's people.' "

King Herod called the wise men. He talked to them about the shining star. "Go to Bethlehem," he said. "Look there for the Baby you seek, who is born to be king of God's people. When you have found him, come and tell me where he is."

Pad, pad, pad, went the camels' feet on the road to little Bethlehem. Tinkle, tinkle, tinkle, went the silver bells that hung from the camels' necks. At last, high in the sky, the wise men saw a bright star shining over a little white house.

The wise men got off their camels and went into the little white house.

And there they found the Baby Jesus with Mary, his mother.

The wise men kneeled down. They opened their treasures and gave precious gifts to the Baby Jesus.

The wise men gave gold, yellow as sunshine. They gave frankincense, sweet-smelling as flowers. They gave myrrh, soft as the finest baby-powder.

And they thanked God for the Baby Jesus.

But the wise men did not go back to Jerusalem to tell King Herod where the Child was, for God sent them home to their own country by another way.

One night Mary and Joseph and little Jesus were fast asleep in the little house in Bethlehem. Joseph was dreaming. In his dream he saw the angel of the Lord.

"Arise," the angel of the Lord told Joseph. "Take the Child and his mother far away into the land of Egypt. For King Herod is trying to hurt little Jesus."

Joseph did not wait. Quickly he awoke Mary, and they got ready for the trip.

Joseph helped Mary on the donkey. She held little Jesus close in her arms. Together Mary and Joseph carried the Child through the friendly dark, far away, down into the land of Egypt, where he was safe from the king who wanted to hurt him. There they lived until there was a new king in Herod's place.

When that time came, the angel of the Lord spoke to Joseph again.

"Arise," he said. "Take the young Child and his mother back to their own land, for the wicked king who wanted to hurt little Jesus is dead."

Mary and Joseph did just as the angel said. They left Egypt and took the Child back to his own country, to the little town of Nazareth.

In Nazareth the Child grew and grew. Sometimes he ran through the narrow little streets and up to the hilltop behind the town. There he could see far away toward the sea. Sometimes he played with other boys and girls, played many games which they all loved. Sometimes he walked straight and tall with a clay jar on his head as he carried water home from the village well. He was strong. He was happy. And he was good. Every day God was helping little Jesus to grow up in the right way.

Twelve Years Old

Birthdays were great times for the boy Jesus just as they are for boys and girls today. Each year he chose from the Bible scroll a verse beginning with the Hebrew letter of his name. He learned every word. That was his birthday verse, his verse to grow on.

At last the day came when Jesus was twelve years old. It was Passover time. Year after year Jesus had watched Mary and Joseph go with the neighbors to the big Temple house in Jerusalem for the Passover service. He had listened as they told of the long tramp over the hills and through the valleys. He had even sung the Passover songs. Often he had shut his eyes and tried to think how the Temple would look as he sang:

"I was glad when they said unto me,
Let us go into the house of the Lord."

This year Jesus, too, could march down the road to Jerusalem. At night, on the way, he could sleep out under the stars with the other pilgrims. Jesus helped his mother prepare the dried dates and the hard bread to eat on the way. He filled the water bag made of dried goatskin. At last it was time to start. Jesus walked tall and straight with the other boys. He listened to all the stories the men told. He stopped with all the rest when they came to the hilltop where they could see Jerusalem and the dome of the Temple shining in the sunlight. And with all the rest Jesus sang:

"I was glad when they said unto me,
Let us go into the house of the Lord."

Jesus walked down the narrow streets and saw the gaily colored stalls in the market places. He could smell the juicy melons and ripe pome-

granates. He watched his mother as she baked the two Passover loaves—one to be taken to the priests at the Temple and the other to be set aside for the family observance. Perhaps Jesus himself carried the loaf as he went with Joseph to the Temple.

On Passover night the family joined in the observance of the feast. Jesus himself asked the question, "What mean you by this service?"

And Joseph told again of the days long ago when the Jews were slaves in Egypt. He told of the deliverer God had sent, and of how Moses had led the chosen people safely across the Red Sea and through the desert and at last brought them to a new homeland.

Then the family sang the Passover hymn together, and Joseph and the Boy went up to the Temple again.

Jesus touched the shining doors. He watched the shadows on the stone floor. He listened to the clear music of the silver horns. He listened to verses from God's Book.

There was one place in the Temple where the Boy liked especially to go. He liked to sit with the great teachers and talk with them about God and the Temple, sometimes to ask questions, sometimes even to answer them.

At last the visit to Jerusalem was over and the Nazareth pilgrims set out for home.

Mary and Joseph had gone a day's trip from the city when they missed Jesus. He was not with the group.

"Have you seen Jesus?" they asked the neighbors and friends. The neighbors and friends shook their heads. No one knew where Jesus was. So Mary and Joseph hurried the long way back to the big city to find him.

"Have you seen Jesus?" they asked in the market place. The merchants shook their heads.

"Have you seen Jesus?" Mary and Joseph asked in the streets. The people shook their heads.

It was three days before Mary and Joseph found Jesus, sitting with the teachers in God's Temple-house, listening to them and asking them questions. And all that heard him were surprised that a boy could know so much.

Mary and Joseph were surprised, too. "Son," Mary said, "Joseph and I have been sad. We were afraid you were lost."

Jesus turned to them. "Did you not know where to find me?" he asked gently. "Did you not know that I would be in my heavenly Father's Temple-house?"

Mary and Joseph did not understand. But they went back to Nazareth, and Jesus went with them.

Back in Nazareth Jesus did just as Mary and Joseph said. Every day he learned more and more. Every day he grew taller and more pleasing to God and to good people.

That is all the Bible tells us about Jesus when he was a boy. But from the things he said and did when he was a man we know a little about those years.

As he grew up in Nazareth, Jesus must have studied and learned Bible verses, for he could repeat many of them word for word.

Jesus must have used his eyes to see birds and flowers and fields. And he learned a great deal from them.

As he grew up in Nazareth, Jesus went to the little synagogue-church. That is what the Bible means when it says that Jesus went to the synagogue on Sabbath days "as his custom was."

Every year Jesus learned more. Every year he grew taller and more pleasing to God. Every year he had another birthday, just as you do.

Jesus increased in wisdom and stature, and in favor with God and man.

When Jesus Grew Up

In Joseph's carpenter shop in Nazareth, the boy Jesus had played about in the curly shavings. He had learned to hammer and saw and to make things. When he grew older, Jesus learned to be a good carpenter just as Joseph had been. He could plane a board, he could build strong wagons and smooth yokes that would not hurt the tender neck of a young ox. People remembered his work in Joseph's shop, for once, years later, when he surprised them with his wise sayings and doings, they asked, "Is not this the carpenter, the son of Mary?"

But even as he worked with his tools, Jesus was thinking and planning the things he would do. He was remembering that God had sent him to be the Saviour.

One day Jesus wiped the shining tools. He put them all away and closed the door of the carpenter shop. He left the little house in Nazareth and walked the long, long miles to the river

Jordan to be baptized by John the Baptist.

John the Baptist shook his head. "I have need to be baptized by you," he told Jesus.

But Jesus knew best. "It is right for you to baptize me," he said.

So John the Baptist baptized Jesus.

As Jesus came up out of the water, God's voice spoke. "This is my beloved Son," God said, "I am well pleased with him."

Jesus went away alone to the wilderness for a while. For forty days and forty nights he stayed there, talking to God and planning his work. He was tired. He was hungry. He was weak for want of food.

One day the tempter came to him. "Change these stones into bread," he said. "If you are really God's Son, you can do that."

But Jesus would not do as the tempter said.
"No," Jesus decided. And he repeated a verse
from God's Book that helped him know right
things to do.

Again the tempter tried to get Jesus to do
wrong. "Jump from the high steeple of the Temple," the devil said. "God will send angels to
take care of you. When you are not hurt, people
will know you are God's son."

Jesus knew that God wanted people to take
care of the bodies he had given them. Again he
shook his head. "No," Jesus said, "God does
not want people to do foolish things to show off."

The tempter tried once more. From the top of
a mountain he showed Jesus all the cities and

towns and countries round about. "These are all mine," the tempter boasted. "I will give them to you if you will kneel down and worship me."

But Jesus shook his head. "No," he said to the tempter. "I will never do that. God's Book says, 'Thou shalt worship the Lord thy God, and him only shalt thou serve.'"

When the tempter saw that Jesus would do no wrong, he went away for a time. He never stopped trying to get Jesus to do wrong. But Jesus never did. The Bible says, *Jesus, the Son of God . . . was in all points tempted like as we are, yet without sin.*

Friendly Jesus

Back by the Jordan River, John the Baptist was still preaching and helping people to be good.

"God's Son has come," John told the people. "He has come to be the Saviour of the world."

One day as Andrew and John were talking with John the Baptist they saw someone going down the road.

"There he is," John said. "There is Jesus about whom I have told you."

Down the road Andrew and John started at once. Step, step, they walked.

Suddenly Jesus stopped. He turned around. "What is it you want?" Jesus asked.

Andrew and John stood still. "Teacher," they said, "where do you live?"

"Come and see," Jesus smiled.

Andrew and John went home with Jesus. They stayed all day with him. They had such a good time. They wished they could stay with Jesus all the time, but they knew they must go home.

Andrew went home to find his brother, Peter.

"I have found Jesus, God's Son," Andrew told Peter. "John and I spent the day with him." And Andrew took Peter with him to meet his new Friend.

Next day in Bethsaida Jesus made more new friends—Philip and Nathanael. "I will teach you to help me in my work," Jesus promised his friends. "You shall see great things as you follow me."

Everywhere Jesus went, he saw people who were sick and needed his help to get well. He saw people who were hungry and needed bread. He saw people who were sad and needed to know God's love. Jesus began to help in every town he visited. People began to talk about Jesus and the wonderful things he did. Great crowds followed him, and the leaders in Jerusalem became jealous, so that for a time Jesus left Judea and went to Galilee.

The road to Galilee led through Samaria, the country most hated by the Jews, and where most of the people hated the Jews.

It was near evening one day when Jesus and his friends came to an old well near the city of Sychar.

Jesus was tired. He sent his friends into the city to buy food while he sat by the well to rest. He could see, outside the city walls, the lovely trees—olive, pear, plum, and walnut. He could smell the almonds and pomegranates ripening on the trees. He could hear the birds singing. Jesus loved to look at the fields. Perhaps he closed his eyes to rest a few minutes and sat quietly, scarcely hearing the blackbird or the lark, as they sang.

Then footsteps broke the stillness of the day and Jesus opened his eyes to see who was coming. It was not his friends returning from the city; they had not time to complete their errand. Nor was it another stranger stopping to rest. It was not even one of his own race whom he saw. It was a Samaritan, a woman, coming down the path from the city, carrying her water jar on her head; coming to the well to draw water.

Jesus looked up into the woman's sad face. "Will you give me a drink, please?" he asked.

The woman stopped short. "You are a Jewish teacher, aren't you?" she questioned. "Yet you are asking a woman of Samaria for water!" She knew the Jews and Samaritans had nothing to do with each other.

Jesus must have smiled. "I will give you something better than water," he promised.

Soon the woman was talking, and Jesus was answering the questions that she asked. "Where is the best place to worship God?" the woman asked. "In the big Temple in the city of Jerusalem, or on the top of that high mountain?"

"You can worship God any place," Jesus explained. "God will listen whenever you speak to him if you are talking from your heart and mean what you say."

129

Happily the woman ran back into the city.

"Come," she told all the people she met. "Come and see this wonderful One. He must be the Saviour whom God promised to send."

The people followed the woman out to the well. "Come into our city," they begged. And Jesus went. For two whole days he stayed in Sychar. And many people there learned to know and love him.

News of his coming reached Galilee before Jesus did. The people crowded to hear him just as they had done in Judea. The synagogues were full of those who listened to his teachings. But Jesus did more than talk. He helped people. He made lame people walk and blind people see. He comforted sad people and taught them of God's love.

One day Jesus went back to Nazareth where he had lived when he was a boy. Just as he had always done, Jesus went to the little synagogue on Sabbath day to worship God. The preacher handed Jesus the Bible book. Jesus took the scroll from its case. He unrolled it and found the place he wanted. He read words something like these:

"'The Lord is with me.

He has sent me to help people who are troubled,
To give sight to blind eyes,
To heal those who are hurt,
To tell people the glad news of his love.'"

Jesus closed the book and gave it back to the preacher. He sat down and all the people listened to hear what he would say.

"This verse in God's Bible book tells about me," Jesus explained. "I will help people who are troubled. I will give sight to blind eyes. I will heal those who are hurt. Everywhere I go, I will tell people the glad news of God's love. Even today I am doing all these things."

The people shook their heads. "Is not this the same Jesus who used to live here?" they asked. They did not believe he had grown to be so great. They were so angry at him that Jesus left the little town he loved. He went away and made for himself a new home in Capernaum.

The-Little-Town-That-Used-To-Be

Capernaum they called it when Jesus lived on earth. It might be called The-Little-Town-That-Used-To-Be. Only the ruins of the village and the broken pillars of the little white synagogue where Jesus preached remain in Palestine today. The houses were white, too, in The-Little-Town-That-Used-To-Be, so white that they fairly shone through the green of the trees and gardens for which the village was famous, long ago.

People today have forgotten a great deal about the trees and flowers but they still remember The-Little-Town-That-Used-To-Be, remember it because of Somebody who lived there for more than a year.

Down by the seaside one day Jesus saw Peter and Andrew casting their nets in the sea, for they were fishermen. "Come and help me in the work that is better than fishing," Jesus called.

Peter and Andrew did not wait, but left their nets and followed Jesus. Farther down on the shore Jesus saw James and John in their boat, mending nets with their father, Zebedee.

"Come and help me in the work that is better than fishing," Jesus called to James and John.

James and John did not wait, but left their nets and the boat and followed Jesus.

Jesus gathered other disciple friends. Day by day he taught them. Day by day they went with him and saw him healing all kinds of sickness and disease.

One Sabbath day, early in the springtime, was a day to remember. Jesus and his disciples had gone to worship God in the little white synagogue. They sat in the seats that were reserved for strangers.

This Person in the stranger's seat had kindness in his face; his hands looked strong and gentle.

The long readings were over and the rabbi turned to the Stranger.

"Will you speak to us this morning?" he said.

The Stranger went to the platform. Everyone listened to his voice and sat very still as he spoke. His words were different than the rabbi's. He spoke not of the old laws and the many, many observances as the rabbis did, but of God the Father and of how he loves the world, and loves little boys and girls, too.

Suddenly there was an interruption.

"What have we to do with thee, Jesus, thou Nazarene? Art thou come to destroy us? I know thee who thou art, the Holy One of God."

It was a man with a bad spirit who spoke.

There was a quick stir. Some were afraid. Some said, "Put the man out."

But Jesus was very quiet. He rebuked the evil spirit within the man.

"Hold thy peace, and come out of him," he said.

There was a struggle. Something inside the man was fighting to hold him from goodness. But Jesus was the stronger. He was stronger than anything that tried to harm one. The evil spirit went out. The man was unhurt.

The Stranger left the synagogue with Simon Peter. He went to Simon Peter's house, very quietly, for Peter's wife's mother was sick with a fever. They had just reached the house when somebody asked Jesus if he would help the sick woman. Jesus was not afraid of disease, just as he was not afraid of the evil spirit in the man. He went to the bedside of the sick woman. Very

gently he touched her hand. Very firmly he rebuked the fever and it left her, and immediately she got up and waited on the family and on its Guest.

It was sunset time. The news of the casting out of the evil spirit had spread over the village. Then there was the rumor that Simon Peter's wife's mother was restored to health. The strict Sabbath laws held the people from unnecessary going to and fro until the sunset hour. Then they hurried to Jesus.

The weak walked slowly as they must because of their illness. A lame boy was on crutches, and others were carried by their friends. The blind were led by their neighbors or felt their way in the darkness. There were some possessed of evil spirits as the man had been. The boys and the girls, too, came running to see Jesus.

The door opened and Jesus came out. Beyond him were the blue waters of Galilee and the sun-lit hills. Around him were the sick, the diseased, the lame, and the blind. But Jesus was not afraid of disease. He loved people in spite of their lameness, in spite of their blindness. He did not wait to tell them why they were sick. He just laid his hand on every one of them and they were healed.

In the Bible there is a picture verse which Jesus' friend, Luke, wrote about that sunset time in The-Little-Town-That-Used-To-Be. It is a picture verse of Jesus.

Now when the sun was setting,
All they that had any sick with divers diseases
Brought them unto him;
And he laid his hands on every one of them,
And healed them.

Busy Days in Capernaum

Everyone was happy one day in the town of Capernaum. Jesus had come home. He had sailed across the blue waters in a fishing boat. He was visiting in the little house down by the sea.

"Jesus has come home!" Men told each other the good news as they went to their work.

"Jesus has come home!" Women told each other the good news as they gathered in the market place.

And the children shouted the good news as they ran to their play—"Jesus has come home!"

Crowds of people came to the little house down by the sea.

There were neighbor men and women and children from all over the little city. There were men and women and children from the country round about. There were wise men from the big cities far away.

The little house down by the sea was full of people. Still the people kept coming to see Jesus. Even the door of the little house was crowded.

Jesus began to preach.

Tramp, tramp, tramp, tramp. Down the street to the little house by the sea came four men. They were carrying a sick man on a pallet bed. The sick man could not walk. His legs shook all the time. They shook so hard that the man could not even stand up. All day long and all night long he had to lie in bed.

"Jesus can make people strong and well," the four friends said. So they carried the sick man to Jesus.

Now the four friends had come to the little house down by the sea. But no one in the crowd moved to let them in.

The four friends waited. They laid down the pallet bed with the sick man on it. Still no one moved to open a way to the door.

At last the four friends thought of the narrow stairs on the outside of the house. They picked up the pallet bed again. Carefully they carried

the sick man up the narrow steps to the flat roof of the little house.

The four friends lifted up part of the roof. They made a big hole. Then they tied ropes to the four corners of the pallet bed.

Down, down, down through the roof, the four friends let the pallet bed until it lay on the floor at Jesus' feet.

Jesus stopped preaching. He looked up at the four men who had found a way to bring their friend to him. He looked down at the man who could not walk.

"Son," Jesus said to the sick man, "your sins are forgiven."

"Did you hear that?" The people looked at Jesus with wonder.

Jesus went on.

"Get up," he said to the man who could not

walk. "Take up your bed and carry it home with you."

The people were looking at the man now. They all saw him stand up. His legs did not shake. They were straight and strong.

The people saw the man pick up his pallet bed. They watched as he carried his bed out the door and down the street. The people were amazed.

"We never saw anything like this," they said to each other.

And they praised God for Jesus.

Wherever Jesus went in Capernaum, the people followed him. Down by the sea they watched one day as he stopped by the table where Matthew the publican was collecting taxes. "Come, follow me," Jesus called to Matthew.

Matthew did not wait. He left his business at once and went to help Jesus in his work.

Matthew wanted all his friends to know Jesus. He gave a great dinner for Jesus one day. All kinds of people were there, rich people and poor people, good people and bad people.

"Look at Jesus," said someone. "He eats with all sorts of people. Some of them are not good, yet he sits at the table with them."

But Jesus did not mind what they said. "People who are good need less help," he said. "I came to help the bad people to become good people."

And all the time Jesus was doing wonderful, kind things. All the time he was healing lame people and sick people and blind people.

In the synagogue one Sabbath day there was a man with a withered right hand.

"Will Jesus heal that man on the Sabbath?" some of the people wondered. For then many people thought it wrong even to help sick people on the Sabbath day, which was the day of rest.

Jesus looked at the man with the poor, useless right hand.

"Come here," Jesus told him.

The man came.

"Stretch forth your right hand," Jesus said.

The man did as he was told. And even as he stretched forth his right hand, it was well and strong again.

There were great and wonderful things to see those busy days when Jesus lived in Capernaum.

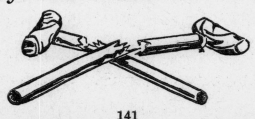

The Great Helper

There was work, much work to be done. There were people to heal and to help and to teach about God's love. So Jesus chose twelve special men to be with him. These he would train to help in his work. Jesus chose Simon to whom he gave the name of Peter. He chose James and John whom he called "Sons of Thunder." He chose steady Andrew, the brother of Peter. He chose Philip whose name meant "one who loves horses," and Bartholomew whom some writers call Nathanael. He chose Matthew, the tax collector, and Thomas. He chose James the son of Alphaeus, sometimes called James the Little. He chose Thaddeus, of whom not much is told, and Simon the Canaanite, a different man from Simon Peter. And Jesus chose Judas, a man of Kerioth.

These Twelve followed Jesus wherever he went. They saw him heal sick and troubled people. They listened to him as he taught about God's love.

One day Jesus took these friends up on a high mountain and told them about God's kingdom of love. He told them the kind of things God wants his people to do. He told them how to be happy.

The things Jesus said that day are called "The Sermon on the Mount." A part of that sermon is the Beatitudes, which you may have learned, the blessed or happy verses.

In his famous Sermon on the Mount Jesus talked about praying. "Remember you are talking to God when you pray," Jesus told his

friends. "Talk to God as you would to a good Father. When you pray, you may say:

"Our Father which art in heaven,
  Hallowed be thy name.
Thy kingdom come.
Thy will be done on earth,
As it is in heaven.
Give us this day our daily bread.
And forgive us our debts,
As we forgive our debtors.
And lead us not into temptation,
But deliver us from evil:
For thine is the kingdom,
And power, and the glory,
  Forever. Amen."

In Palestine today on the side of a mountain called "Little Hermon" there is a poor little village called Nain. The people who live there are not proud of their town, but they show visitors the great rock tombs which have been outside the town since the days when Jesus lived on earth. Nain must have been different then, a busy place with flowers and fruit and many people. Perhaps it even deserved its name, which means "beautiful."

One day a great crowd of people followed Jesus and his twelve friends as they came near the village of Nain. At the city gate they could hear the slow, sad notes of funeral music played on flutes. They could hear the slow, sad songs of the mourners who always followed the dead.

Inside the gate Jesus and his disciples met a funeral procession. There were the bearers of the dead. There was the weeping mother whose only son had just died. The father was not there, for he had died long ago. And there were many people who had come to try to comfort the mother.

Jesus stopped. "Do not cry," he said to the mother. Then, to the dead man he said, "Young man, I say unto thee, arise."

Immediately the dead man sat up and began to speak. And his mother and his friends praised God for the wonderful things that had been done. The flutes began to play glad music. The people began to sing glad songs. Then it was a happy procession that walked the streets of Nain.

About this time Jesus' friend, John the Baptist, was in prison. King Herod had put him there when John had accused the king of doing evil deeds. For Herod had been wicked.

It had been some time since John had seen Jesus. He sent messengers to ask a question.

"Are you really the Saviour King whom God promised to send?" they asked Jesus. "John the Baptist wants to know."

Jesus did not answer right away. Instead he let John's messengers watch him work. They saw him heal many who were sick. They saw him cast evil spirits out of people. They saw him give sight to eyes that had been blind. Then Jesus gave them a message.

"Go your way," Jesus said. "Go and tell John the things you have seen and heard. Tell him that the blind receive their sight, and the lame walk, the lepers are cleansed, and the deaf hear, and the dead are raised up, and the poor have the gospel preached to them."

The men went back to John. They told what they had seen and heard. And John was satisfied.

But the enemies of Jesus, many of them scribes and Pharisees, were not glad for these things. They grew more and more envious of Jesus. They grew more and more angry because the people loved to hear Jesus and be with him. They even accused Jesus of being evil.

Jesus knew that people needed to know about God and his way of love. He knew that they needed a Saviour. He knew, too, that there was work, much work, to be done. Day by day he taught his disciples, sometimes in the fields, sometimes on the mountain, sometimes down by the sea. Sometimes he taught them using verses from the Old Testament. Sometimes he taught them using stories. Sometimes he spoke of the birds and the flowers and the fish. But always he was helping his disciples to understand God and his love. He was teaching them so that they, too, could do God's work upon the earth.

By Galilee

It was evening time. The sun was turning the blue waters of the lake pink and silver. Jesus and his disciples were talking. "Let us get into the boat and row across the lake," Jesus said.

The disciple friends nodded. They got the boat ready. Soon it was skimming over the waters.

Lap, lap, the waters rocked the little boat gently like a cradle. Soon Jesus was asleep.

Lap, lap, the waves rocked the little boat gently like a cradle. Everything was still and quiet.

Suddenly there came a storm. The wind blew hard. The clouds were dark and heavy. The waves rolled high. The water splashed into the boat. Harder blew the wind. Blacker grew the clouds. Bigger rolled the waves. The boat was filling with water.

The disciples turned to Jesus. "Wake up," they begged. "Wake up. We are afraid."

Jesus opened his eyes. Tall and straight he stood up in the boat and held his hand out over the stormy waters.

Jesus spoke to the wind. "Peace. Be still," he told the wind.

Jesus spoke to the water. "Peace. Be still," he told the water.

The wind stopped blowing. The waves stopped rolling. The dark clouds went away. The waters lay smooth and quiet. All was still. There was no sound but the soft lap, lap of the waves that rocked the boat gently like a cradle.

The disciples looked at the quiet water. They looked at Jesus.

They said to each other, "Even the wind and the waters do as Jesus says."

One day Jesus was on a boat sailing across the blue waters of Galilee. In a city by the sea the people must have heard the good news, for they were waiting to welcome him. When the

boat landed, a man stepped out of the crowd and kneeled down at Jesus' feet.

"It is Jairus!" someone whispered, "Jairus, the head of the synagogue."

"My little daughter!" Jairus could hardly speak the words. "My little daughter is even now dead. Please come and lay your hands on her that she may live again."

Jesus turned and followed Jairus. As they pressed through the crowd, a woman who had been sick for twelve years pushed her way to them. Timidly she reached out her hand and touched the hem of Jesus' long coat.

"If I can only touch him, even his robe, I shall get well," she thought. "I know I shall."

And she was right. Immediately she was well.

Jesus felt the woman's light touch.

"Who touched me?" he asked.

The woman fell at his feet. Was he angry? she wondered.

But Jesus said: "Be of good cheer, my daughter. Your faith has made you strong and well again."

And he went on his way.

At last Jairus's house was in sight. Jesus saw crowds of people. He heard the slow, sad music of the funeral flute players. "It is no use," some-one said. "The child is dead."

But Jesus walked on. "Do not be afraid," he told Jairus. "Just trust me."

Through the crowd Jesus made his way. Then, taking James and John and Peter and Jairus and the little girl's mother, he went into the bedroom.

Gently Jesus took the dead child by the hand. "Little girl," he said, "it's time to get up."

And the little girl arose and walked.

"Give her something to eat," Jesus told the mother and father. As he left the house, he heard the sad music change to glad music. He saw smiles instead of tears. He heard the happy voices of Jairus and his friends.

As Jesus passed down the street, two blind men followed him. Jesus healed them.

Then a man who could not talk was brought to Jesus. Jesus healed him and he spoke again. No matter what the trouble, Jesus could help. The Great Helper never failed.

A Boy's Lunch

One day Jesus decided to let his friends try some of the special work they had seen him do. Calling the Twelve to him, he sent them out, two by two, into all the cities and villages round about. He gave them power over sicknesses and over evil spirits.

Out the Twelve went, two by two, to spread the gospel of God's love just as Jesus was doing. It was a wonderful trip. When they returned, all the disciples were anxious to tell Jesus what they had done. They came together near Bethsaida to talk about it.

"Let's sail across the lake and rest a while," Jesus suggested.

The disciples smiled. They always loved a day alone with Jesus. Quickly they got into a little boat and sailed away.

But there were other people near Bethsaida that day who came to hear Jesus. They had missed him and followed after him. There were crowds of them. And there was a boy. The boy saw the crowd and followed it. Tramp, tramp, tramp, the people hurried down the path that led around the little lake of blue water. The boy could hardly keep up with them. He did not quite understand what was going on, but the people were talking and pointing to the water.

"There is the boat!" a man shouted. "There is the boat, and Jesus and his disciples are in it!"

The boy looked. He could see the white sails dipping into the blue water of the lake. He could see men in the boat.

"You will see wonderful things today, if you come with us," a man in the crowd told the boy. "This Jesus has cured sick people all over the country. He has made lame people strong. He has even opened the eyes of blind people."

The boy did not answer. He was not lame, or blind, or sick. He held on a bit tighter to the little basket in his hand. He would eat those five barley loaves and two small fishes later. Now he must keep up with the crowd. He did not want to miss anything.

Tramp, tramp, tramp, the people walked faster. The boy walked faster, too. The crowd was almost around the little lake now.

"We'll get there before the boat does," one man said.

And sure enough, the people were resting on the ground when the little boat pulled up to shore.

The crowd began to shout. "There he is," they cried. "There is Jesus!"

And there was Jesus climbing out of the boat with his twelve disciple friends.

Jesus looked at the people. He looked at his disciple friends. His friends understood that there would be no happy time alone with Jesus this day. There were people who needed him.

He led them up the hill a little way to a place where green grass was growing. Then He turned to the people.

He healed people who were sick. He cured people who were lame. He told them about God and his love. All day Jesus was teaching, and healing, and helping the people. The boy had never seen anything so wonderful before.

Evening drew near. At sunset time one of the disciples came to Jesus.

"Master," he whispered, "send these people away. The day is gone and they have had nothing

to eat. Send them into the towns and country places to buy bread for themselves."

The boy heard, and looked for his basket. He had forgotten all about those five barley loaves and two small fishes.

He watched Jesus' face. He listened to hear what Jesus would say.

"The people need not go away," Jesus told the disciple. "You give them something to eat."

The disciple friend shook his head. "We have no food to give," he said. "Shall we try to buy bread for such a crowd? There are five thousand men besides the women and children. It would take a lot of money to give each one even a bite."

Jesus was speaking again. "See how much food there is here," he told his disciple friends.

The boy guessed the answer even before Andrew said the words. "There is a boy here who has five barley loaves and two small fishes."

Andrew stopped. Then he added, "But what are they among so many?"

Jesus looked at the crowd. "Tell the people to sit down on the green grass," he said. "Have them sit together—fifty or a hundred of them together."

The boy saw the disciples pass among the people. Soon the crowd was dotted with the bright-colored robes of men and women and children.

The boy turned away from the people and looked up to find Jesus looking straight into his eyes. Jesus held out his hand.

"May I have your lunch?" he asked.

The boy nodded. He held up the little basket. Then he stood quite still and waited.

Jesus took the five small barley loaves and held them in his hands. He looked up at the sunset sky. He blessed the bread and broke it and gave it to the disciples.

"Give bread to all the people," Jesus said.

The disciple friends took the bread. They passed among the people and gave bread to all.

Jesus took the two small fishes and held them in his hands. He looked up at the sunset sky. He blessed the fishes and broke them and gave them to the disciples.

"Give fish to all the people," Jesus said.

The disciple friends took the fish. They passed among the people and gave fish to each one. Never had bread and fish tasted so good, the boy thought.

When everybody had had enough to eat, Jesus spoke again. "Gather up the bread that is left," he said to his disciple friends. "Let nothing be wasted."

And the disciples gathered up twelve baskets full of broken loaves.

The people laughed and shouted. "We will make Jesus king of our country," they said. But Jesus shook his head. He did not want to be king of a country. He wanted to be a king of love and rule in the hearts of people. He started his disciples back to Bethsaida in the little boat. And Jesus himself went up into the mountain to pray.

God's Beloved Son

By what he did, by what he said, by the things he helped his friends to do and to say, Jesus kept on teaching.

Then, one day, Jesus gave his disciples a test. Of one thing they must be very sure, if they would carry on his work. Jesus would help them to know that thing. "Who do men say that I am?" he asked as they walked along.

The disciples told what they had heard. "Some say John the Baptist," they said. "Some say Elijah, some Jeremiah, some say other of the old prophets."

Now came the important question. "But who do you say that I am?" Jesus asked.

Just as he always did, Peter answered first. "Thou art the Christ, the Son of the living God," Peter said. The others nodded.

"So I am, Peter," Jesus said. "The Heavenly Father helped you to know that. This truth that I am God's Son is the key to the door of heaven. This truth is yours to share."

But he charged his disciples to tell this to no man at this time.

Then Jesus began to tell his disciples some sad things. The chief priests and the scribes would reject him, he said. They would kill him, but after three days he would rise again.

"No! No!" Peter almost shouted the words. "Such a thing must never be!"

"You do not understand," Jesus told Peter. "People who live according to God's love must not think of themselves. They must do hard things and help people. Whosoever would save his life shall lose it; and whosoever shall lose his life for my sake shall find it."

The disciples did not understand. But they were learning more every day from the Great Teacher. Every day Jesus tried to help the Twelve to understand something of the hardships and sorrows which must come to them.

One day, as the setting sun tinted the clouds with long rays of crimson and silver light, Jesus spoke.

"Come," he said to Peter, James, and John, "let us go up on the mountain."

Together the four climbed the grassy slopes.

Together they watched the sunset fade from the west. Then the quiet darkness came and the tired disciples were soon drowsy with sleep.

But Jesus was not sleepy. He was praying to his Father.

As he talked with his Father, something of the glory that he had had in heaven was his again. His face shone as the sun. His garments became white and dazzling in their brightness. Beside him stood two men, Moses the lawgiver, and Elijah the prophet. They had come back to earth, to talk to Jesus about his death, by which he would save the world.

The vision drove away all thought of sleep from the weary disciples. Perhaps they thought it was a dream. But when they were fully awake, they saw his glory, and the two men that stood with him. None of them understood it, but they knew it was wonderful and they wanted it to last.

"Let us make three leafy tenthouses here," said Peter, "one for our Master, one for Moses, and one for Elijah." Was it his idea that they would camp out there upon the mountain with Jesus?

Yet, even as he spoke a bright cloud came down upon the mountain, and from the cloud there came a voice saying: "This is my beloved Son, in whom I am well pleased; hear ye him." It was the voice of God himself.

The disciples were afraid. They fell on the ground and hid their faces.

But Jesus understood the glory. He understood his disciples, too, just as he always did.

"Arise, be not afraid," Jesus said. He came to them and touched them. It was the dear voice that they loved. It was their own Master's hand. They lifted their eyes and "saw no one, save Jesus only," Jesus the Son of God.

Together Jesus and Peter and James and John walked down the mountain to meet the other disciples.

Good Answers to Every Question

Jesus and his disciples were on their way to Capernaum. Again Jesus was trying to prepare his friends for the things that would happen so soon.

"The Son of man shall be delivered into the hands of cruel men," Jesus said. "They shall kill him, but God will raise him up the third day."

The disciples could not understand, but they were sad. And somehow they could not find words to ask the questions that were in their hearts.

Back in Capernaum where Jesus had made his home for nearly three years, a tax collector came to Peter.

"Doesn't this Teacher of yours pay the half-shekel tax?" he asked.

Peter nodded. He knew Jesus always paid his debts. Had he forgotten? Peter wondered.

Jesus answered his unspoken question when they were together.

"You had better go down to the sea and fish

a bit," he told Peter. "Take up the first fish you catch. When you open his mouth you will find a silver piece of money in it. Take it and pay both my taxes and your own."

It was later that the disciples came to Jesus, asking, "Who will be greatest in the kingdom of heaven?" for they had been disputing about that as they walked along the road. Jesus sat down and called the Twelve close to him. Then he took a little child and set him by his side. "Whosoever shall be humble as this child is humble, he shall be greatest in the kingdom of heaven," Jesus explained.

Question after question the disciples asked. And Jesus answered every one. Peter brought his question last.

"Lord," Peter asked, "how often must I forgive my brother if he hurts me? Seven times is enough, isn't it?"

Jesus looked straight at Peter. He saw the hurt deep down in Peter's heart. He saw the hot anger that was there. But Jesus saw something else, too. He saw how fine Peter could be, if he only understood.

Jesus shook his head. "No, Peter," Jesus said

gently, "seven times is not enough. We must go on forgiving whenever there is need, even seventy times seven." Then Jesus told Peter and the other disciples a story to help them understand what he meant.

"Once upon a time," Jesus began, "there lived a king with many servants. One day there was brought to him a servant who owed him a great deal of money. The servant had nothing with which to pay, and the law said that he and his wife and his children and all he had should be sold for the debt. The servant fell on his knees before the king.

" 'Have mercy on me,' the servant begged. 'Give me time and I will pay the whole debt.' The king agreed.

"Then the servant went out and found another servant who owed him seventeen dollars. Roughly he grabbed the man by the throat. 'Pay me all you owe me,' he demanded.

" 'Have mercy on me,' the servant begged. 'Give me time and I will pay the whole debt.'

"But the servant would not have mercy on the one who owed him that little debt. He had him put into prison.

"The other servants of the king were watching. Quickly they ran to tell the king, who sent for his servant. 'You are a wicked man,' the king said. 'I forgave you all the debt which you owed me. Should you not have forgiven your fellow-servant even as I forgave you?'

"And the king sent the unforgiving servant out to be punished."

Peter had his answer in two ways—in plain words and in a story.

The disciples had a chance very soon to see how Jesus himself would act when people were not nice to him. On the way to Jerusalem the road led through an unfriendly country where the Samaritans lived.

It was evening time when Jesus and his friends came near a little village, and Jesus sent messengers ahead to find a place to spend the night. Now the Samaritans did not like the Jews. They did not like people to go to the city of Jerusalem. They would not let Jesus and his friends come into their city to spend the night. The messengers brought back this news to their Master.

James and John were angry. "Let us call down fire from heaven and destroy this village," they begged Jesus.

But Jesus shook his head. "You do not understand," he said. "The Son of man came not to destroy and hurt men, but to heal and to help them." And quietly Jesus led his disciples to another village.

One morning as Jesus was teaching in Jerusalem some men brought to him a woman who had sinned.

"Master," they said, "this woman has been very, very bad. The law says that she should be stoned to death. What do you say?"

They waited.

For a moment Jesus did not say a word. Instead, he stooped down, and with his finger wrote something in the sand.

Again the men asked their question.

Jesus straightened up. Then he spoke. "Let the one of you who has never done a bad thing cast the first stone," he said.

And again Jesus stooped down, and with his finger wrote in the sand.

One by one the waiting men slipped away,

ashamed, and Jesus and the woman were left alone.

Jesus looked up.

"Where are those who wanted to hurt you?" he asked the woman. "Did none of them punish you?"

The woman did not lift her eyes. "No man, Lord," she said.

Again Jesus spoke. "Neither do I punish thee," he said. "Go, and do not do bad things any more."

Jesus was always ready to help those who asked. There was no question too hard for him to answer.

Neighbors

There was still much work to be done, more than Jesus and his twelve special friends could find time to touch. One day Jesus chose seventy others and sent them out two by two to visit the cities and country places.

"Tell the people about God and his way of love," Jesus commanded these seventy. "Help sick people and sad people just as I have done."

The seventy went out. One day they came back. "Lord," they shouted, "even the evil spirits do as we say."

Jesus was glad for every good thing that his friends did. He thanked the heavenly Father for all the good work they had done.

Still people brought their questions to Jesus. It was a lawyer who asked one day, "Master, what shall I do to have eternal life?"

"You know the law," Jesus replied. "What is it?"

The lawyer knew the old law. He could repeat it without missing a word.

" 'Thou shalt love the Lord thy God with all thy heart, and with all thy soul,' he began, 'and with all thy strength, and with all thy mind, and thy neighbor as thyself.' "

"That is right," Jesus said. "Can you love God and your neighbors that way?"

But the lawyer had another question. "Who is my neighbor?" he asked.

And Jesus answered with a story that is famous all over the world today. Here it is in the very words of the Bible.

A certain man went down from Jerusalem to Jericho, and fell among thieves, which stripped him of his raiment, and wounded him, and departed, leaving him half dead.

And by chance there came down a certain priest that way: and when he saw him, he passed by on the other side.

And likewise a Levite, when he was at the

place, came and looked on him, and passed by on the other side.

But a certain Samaritan, as he journeyed, came where he was: and when he saw him, he had compassion on him,

And went to him, and bound up his wounds, pouring in oil and wine, and set him on his own beast, and brought him to an inn, and took care of him.

And on the morrow when he departed, he took out two pence, and gave them to the host, and said unto him, Take care of him; and whatsoever thou spendest more, when I come again, I will repay thee. — Luke 10:30–35.

When the story was all finished, Jesus asked, "Which of these three men do you think was neighbor unto him that fell among thieves?"

That was easy. "The man who helped him," the lawyer said.

"Go, and do thou likewise," Jesus said.

The Little Old Lady

It was the Sabbath day in Capernaum, and time to go to the synagogue to worship God. A little old lady reached for the stick she needed to help her walk. Slowly, oh, so slowly, she pulled herself to her feet. But she did not stand tall and straight as you do. She stood all bent over, for the little old lady had a crooked back.

There had been a time when the little old lady had stood tall and straight, but that was long years ago. For eighteen long years the little old lady had had a crooked back.

Slowly, oh, so slowly, the little old lady hobbled down the steps. She started down the street. As she walked her stick made a little tap, tap, tapping sound.

There had been a time when the little old lady had walked fast down the street to the synagogue-church, but that was long years ago. For eighteen long years the little old lady had had a crooked back.

Now the little old lady climbed the steps of

the synagogue-church. Slowly, oh, so slowly, she went up those steps, for climbing hurt her.

Slowly, oh, so slowly, the little old lady walked into the synagogue-church and sat down.

"There is a new teacher today," someone whispered to the little old lady. "His name is Jesus."

She tried to see the new teacher, but it was hard to lift her head with her poor back all bent over.

Still, she could hear. She turned her head to listen as Jesus talked about God and his love.

Suddenly Jesus stopped talking and he looked straight at the little old lady. "Come here and stand by me," Jesus said.

The little old lady did not wait. She reached for her stick. As fast as her poor, crooked back would let her, the little old lady got on her feet and went tap, tap, tapping across the room to Jesus. There she stood quite still.

Jesus leaned down. Gently he put his two kind hands on the little old lady's crooked back. He spoke to her.

"Woman," Jesus said, "today your poor, crooked back is straight and strong. It will not hurt any more."

The little old lady straightened up. Her stick fell to the floor. Tall and straight she stood and looked into the face of Jesus. Then she began to praise God.

And many people thanked God for the kind things Jesus did.

But the head of the synagogue began to complain because of the thing Jesus had done. "There are six days in which people ought to work," he said. "This woman could have been healed another day. Healing is work, and should not be done on the Sabbath."

Jesus was ready with an answer. "You water your horse on the Sabbath, do you not?" he asked. "Isn't it more important to help a woman who has suffered for eighteen years?"

And the crowds rejoiced.

Jesus and the Children

Step, step, step, some children and their mothers walked down the road. Some of the children were big boys and girls. They walked tall and straight with long, long steps. They were on their way to see Jesus. Some of the children were little ones. They skipped along with short, short steps. They were on their way to see Jesus. Some of the children were just tiny babies in their mothers' arms. The babies could not walk even one step. But the mothers could walk. Step, step, step, the mothers carried their babies to see Jesus.

As they walked down the road, the mothers sang.

"We are going to see Jesus," the mothers sang. "We are glad."

"We are going to see Jesus," the big boys and girls sang. "We are glad."

"We are going to see Jesus," the little children sang. "We are glad."

And the tiny babies made soft, little noises

that sounded like a song: "We are going to see Jesus. We are glad."

"We want our children to see Jesus," the mothers told each other. "We want Jesus to put his kind hands on our children and bless them."

On they went walking down the road, step, step, step—the big boys and girls, the little children, and the mothers carrying their babies. They were going to see Jesus.

At last they saw some people.

"There is Jesus," someone said. "All those men are talking to him."

The mothers and their children went on down the road. But before they could get to Jesus, some men stopped them.

"Jesus is busy," the men said. "You cannot see him. Take your children away."

The mothers turned away. The children turned away. Slowly, slowly, they started down the road. This time they were not singing.

Then the children heard Jesus talking.

"Let the children come to me," Jesus was telling the men. "Do not send them away. My heavenly Father loves little children, and I love them, too."

The little children turned and ran to Jesus. The big boys and girls ran. Even the mothers ran, holding their tiny babies close in their arms.

The men stood to one side.

Straight to Jesus the little children and their mothers went.

Jesus smiled at the children. He put his arms around the big boys and girls. He held the little children close. He took the babies in his arms.

Jesus talked to God about the children. He laid his hands on them and blessed them. "My heavenly Father loves children," Jesus said, "and I love you, every one."

Step, step, step, the children and their mothers went walking down the road again. Some of the children were big boys and girls. They were walking tall and straight with long, long steps. They had been to see Jesus. Some of the children were little ones. They were skipping along with short, short steps. They had been to see Jesus. Some of the children were just tiny babies in their mothers' arms. The babies could not walk even one step. But the mothers could walk. Step, step, step, the mothers had carried their babies to see Jesus.

As they walked down the road, the mothers began to sing. They sang a happy song:

"We have been to see Jesus,
We are glad, glad, glad!"

The big boys and girls began to sing. They sang a happy, happy song:

"We have been to see Jesus,
We are glad, glad, glad!"

The little children began to sing. They sang a happy, happy song:

"We have been to see Jesus,
We are glad, glad, glad!"

And the tiny babies made soft, little noises that sounded like a happy song:

"We have been to see Jesus,
We are glad, glad, glad!"

A Man Who Said Thank You

There were ten sick men who lived all alone outside a little town. They could not go to their homes, for their families might get sick, too. They could not go to the houses next door to their homes, for the neighbors might get sick. They could not go places with their friends, for their friends might get sick.

No doctor could make the ten sick men well. They must live all alone on the outskirts of the little town.

"We wish we could go home," the ten sick men often said to each other. "We wish we could go home to see our families. We wish we could go to see the neighbors. We wish we could see our friends inside the town."

But the ten sick men could not go home. They had to live all alone outside the town.

One day the ten sick men heard news.

"There is a man who makes people well of sickness like yours," someone who dared to come near told them. "His name is Jesus."

The ten sick men listened to the news. Then they shook their heads.

"We could never find Jesus," the sick men said. "We cannot go inside the town to hunt for him."

One day as they sat by the side of the road they heard footsteps. They saw people. Then they heard a shout.

"Jesus is coming!" someone shouted.

The ten sick men jumped to their feet. As loud as they could, they called to Jesus.

"Please make us well," the sick men begged.

Jesus looked at them. He knew how much they wanted to go home to their families. He knew how much they wanted to go to see the neighbors. He knew how much they wanted to be with friends inside the town.

"Go into the town," Jesus told the ten sick men. "Go, and show yourselves to the doctor."

The ten sick men did not wait. At once they started running into the town. And as they ran, they saw that the sores on their hands were all gone. The sores on their feet and on their bodies were all gone. The ten sick men were well.

One man stopped right where he was. He turned around and ran back to Jesus. He kneeled down at Jesus' feet. He bowed his head. He said:

"Thank you,
Thank you,
Thank you,
Jesus."

Jesus looked at the man who had been so sick. He looked far down the road and saw nine other men running into the town.

"Were not ten men made well?" Jesus asked.

Then Jesus smiled at the man who had come back to say thank you.

"Go home to your family and friends," Jesus told the man. "I am glad you are well."

Tap, tap, the man's feet made glad little sounds as they went running in to the little town. Over and over again they seemed to tap, tap the words:

Thank you,
Thank you,
Thank you,
Jesus.

Into the City

"Will Jesus come?"

All Jerusalem was asking the question. It was just before the great Feast of the Passover.

"If he does we shall be ready. It will be the last of him who will not keep our rules," a high priest said.

"This Jesus cleansed a leper," said a pilgrim from the seacoast country. "His skin was as clear and smooth as my own."

"And he brings light to many sightless eyes," added a Galilean.

"Even from the dead he brought back Lazarus!" It was one of the early comers from Bethany speaking. "I myself saw him walk out from the tomb."

"The Pharisees are plotting to hurt Jesus." It was a boy speaking, a boy who lived near the Temple. "They want to kill him. I heard them give orders that he be taken if he dared come near the city."

Back in Bethany Jesus and the Twelve had

rested for a little while with Mary, Martha, and Lazarus. Then they joined the other pilgrims on their journey.

At the foot of the Mount of Olives, near Bethphage, the travelers stopped for a while.

"Go into the city," said Jesus to two of his disciples. "There you will find a colt tied; loose him and bring him to me. If anyone asks you why you do this, say, 'The Lord needs him,' and it will be all right."

The disciples obeyed. Entering the village, they found the colt just as Jesus had said. Folding their garments, they made a kind of saddle and brought the colt to Jesus.

The pilgrim band had waited with Jesus. As they saw the Teacher from Nazareth mount the colt, they remembered the stories of other days, stories of Jewish kings who rode on errands of peace on the backs of colts. They remembered that it was down this same valley that Solomon had ridden on King David's mule to sit on David's throne. Could it be that at last the promised King was coming?

Excitement grew as the crowds came down the road to Jerusalem.

"There he is!" the men said. "There is Jesus who took five loaves and two small fishes and fed five thousand men."

"There he is!" the women told each other. "There is Jesus who cured the little old lady with a crooked back."

"There he is!" the children shouted. "There is Jesus who put his hands on our heads and talked to God about us."

The men were singing. The women were singing. The children were singing.

All the people were singing together:

"Praise, praise to God,

We thank him for Jesus!"

The people sang, and shouted. They waved leafy branches of the trees. Some of them took off their coats and made a carpet on the dusty road. For Jesus was riding by.

The people watched as Jesus went on down the road and stopped at the beautiful Temple. They followed him inside.

In the Temple there were blind people who could not see. Jesus made their eyes well.

In the Temple there were lame people who could not walk. Jesus made their legs well.

In the Temple there were sad people who did not smile. Jesus told them about God and his way of love.

When Jesus stopped speaking, it was very quiet.

Suddenly there was a sound in the Temple. The children were singing:

"Praise, praise to God,
We thank him for Jesus!"

The children sang the words over and over.

"Don't you hear that noise?" a man asked Jesus.

But Jesus was smiling as he listened to the children.

"The children's songs are the sweetest music in all the world," Jesus told the man.

The children had not heard. They were looking at Jesus. They were still singing their song of love:

"Praise, praise to God,
We thank him for Jesus!"

All the city was talking about Jesus. They were telling of his teachings, of his kindness, of his healing the sick and the lame.

But Jesus slipped quietly away and went back to Bethany. There he rested in the home of Mary and Martha and Lazarus.

The Lovely Lady

In the village of Bethany, where Jesus stayed so often with his friends, lived a lovely lady. Her name was Mary. It was Mary's brother, Lazarus, whom Jesus had raised from the dead.

One day the lovely lady was invited to a dinner party. It was a dinner party for her friend, Jesus.

Mary wanted something very much. She did not want a dress for the party. She did not want shoes for the party. She only wanted a beautiful present for her friend, Jesus.

The lovely lady looked at her pretty things on the table. She shook her head. "Not one of them is nice enough for Jesus," she said.

The lovely lady looked at all her pretty things in the room. She shook her head. "Not one of them is nice enough for Jesus," she said.

Then the lovely lady thought of something she had had for a long, long time. It was so nice that she kept it put away. The lovely lady liked it best of all the pretty things she had. It was a jar of fine perfume, sweet-smelling like flowers. The jar was shining and smooth. The lovely lady liked to hold it in her hand, and she liked the perfume that was sweet-smelling like flowers.

"I will take my shining jar of sweet perfume to Jesus," she said.

The day came for the dinner party. Mary got out her shining jar of sweet perfume. She held it tightly in her hand as she walked to the dinner party. Her feet made a happy little tap, tap, tap on the ground.

At the dinner party there were many men at the table with Jesus. The lovely lady slipped into the room. Inside the door she stopped. She was holding the shining jar of sweet perfume tightly in her hand. She waited a moment.

Then she walked softly to the seat where Jesus was. She opened the smooth, shining jar and poured the perfume on Jesus' feet and wiped them with her hair. The whole room was sweet-smelling like flowers.

The men spoke first. "Look at this woman!" they grumbled. "She is pouring out perfume that could be sold for much money."

But Jesus was smiling.

"It is a beautiful present the lovely lady has given me," he told everyone at the dinner party. "All over the world, wherever people hear of me, they shall hear the story of the lovely lady and her beautiful gift."

Judas was one of the men who had not liked the gift Mary brought to Jesus. When the dinner party was over, he slipped out to talk with the enemies of Jesus. And he promised to help them get Jesus, if they would promise to give him thirty pieces of silver money.

A Supper to Remember

It was the day for the Passover meal, and Jesus had sent Peter and John to prepare a room where he and his disciples might eat supper together.

Peter and John were glad to help Jesus. They found a large upstairs room in the home of one of Jesus' friends. There they prepared the thin bread, the lamb seasoned with bitter herbs, and the fruit wine that was always used at Passover time.

That night Jesus and his disciples came for the feast. They were tired, and their feet were soiled with the dust that sifted through their open sandals. There was usually a servant to wash the feet of guests when they came into a house, but Peter and John had not provided for that. Perhaps they thought that the owner of the house would send his servant. But none came. What a chance for one of the disciples to help! But not a disciple moved from his seat.

It was Jesus himself who got up from the

table, laid aside his long coat, and tied a towel around his waist. Then he poured fresh water into a bowl and began to wash a disciple's feet and wipe them with the towel which hung from the waist. From one disciple to another he went.

No one said a word until Jesus came to Peter.

"Lord," Peter blurted out, "I can't let you wash my feet."

Jesus spoke gently. "If you belong to me, I must wash your feet." And he washed Peter's feet along with the rest.

When Jesus had finished, he put on his coat, and sat down again. Then he said: "I have given you an example, that you should do as I have done. No one is too good to do anything that needs to be done."

At last the Passover meal was over.

The table was almost empty. There remained only some of the bread and wine. Judas had gone out to betray the Son of God. Jesus and the eleven friends were lingering for a last talk together.

Jesus had told them that he would not eat the feast again with them, that the time of his death was at hand. They looked at him sorrowfully.

As they looked, he took the bread in his hand. He bowed his head in blessing, giving thanks. Then he broke the bread and passed it to his friends. "Take, eat," he said, "this is my body which is given for you. This do in remembrance of me."

The plate passed from hand to hand. There was silence in the upper room as they sat together with their eyes on Jesus.

Then Jesus took the cup. Again he bowed his head and the disciples heard him give thanks.

"Drink of it, all of you," he said, "for this is my blood of the new covenant which is shed for many that their sins may be forgiven."

The disciples drank wonderingly. As they finished, Jesus said, "This do, as oft as ye drink it, in remembrance of me."

They were puzzled. They were sorrowful. But again Jesus was speaking.

"Let not your heart be troubled," he said, "believe in God, believe likewise in me. In my Father's house are many mansions; if it were not so, I would have told you. I go to prepare a place for you. And if I go and prepare a place for you, I come again, and will receive you unto myself; that where I am, there ye may be also."

The little company stood up. Together they sang the last Passover hymn:

"Oh, give thanks unto the Lord; for he is good,
For his loving kindness endureth forever."

Then they went, Jesus and the eleven friends, out toward the Mount of Olives.

In an Old Garden

On a little hill outside the walls of Jerusalem there is a beautiful garden. Inside the garden are olive trees, gnarled and old. It is called the Garden of Gethsemane.

Together Jesus and his friends had walked quietly through the streets of Jerusalem. And Jesus talked to them of his plans, and of his promise to come to them again. Then they had entered the garden.

Most of the company waited a little way inside the gate. Jesus was sad. He wanted his best friends with him. So he asked Peter and James and John to go part of the way with him.

"Watch ye here," he said to them at last, "while I go yonder and pray."

Then, alone, Jesus talked to his Father about his coming death.

When he returned to the three, they were fast asleep. But Jesus understood that his friends were tired.

"Sleep on now, and take your rest," he said.

Their sleep was not for long. Soon they could see a mob approaching with the soldiers who had come to arrest Jesus. Together Jesus and eleven friends went to meet the soldiers. The lanterns and torches shining through the gray olive leaves showed a crowd carrying swords and staves.

As they drew nearer, Jesus stepped forward and came face to face with Judas.

"Master," said Judas, and kissed him, for this was the sign on which he had agreed that the soldiers might know Jesus.

"Friend," there was sorrow in Jesus' voice, "do you betray the Son of man with a kiss?"

Then to the mob he said, quietly, "Whom seek ye?"

"Jesus of Nazareth," they muttered.

"I am he," said Jesus.

The soldiers came forward to arrest him.

Quickly Peter drew his sword and struck at them, cutting off one man's ear; but Jesus told him to put up his sword. Gently he touched the hurt ear and healed it.

"Don't you know," he questioned Peter, "that I could ask my Father and he would send thou-

sands of angels to protect me? But if I did, how should God's promises in the Scriptures be fulfilled?"

Pointing to his disciples, Jesus said to the soldiers, "Let these men who are with me go."

Then all the disciples left him and fled. Fled, leaving Jesus to face his enemies alone!

Peter and John, too, fled, but they could not stay away. Slipping along behind the mob in the darkness, they saw the soldiers take Jesus to the house of Annas, the high priest. John was known there and at a word from him the maid admitted Peter. He did not follow John into the house, but stayed with the crowd about the fire in the courtyard, outside.

Even there he could hear the false witnesses as they swore that Jesus had blasphemed the

Temple, Jesus who had driven the traders from his Father's house! He could hear them accuse Jesus of disloyalty to the government, Jesus, who had said, "Render therefore unto Caesar the things that are Caesar's."

"Art thou the Christ?" Peter heard them ask.

Would Jesus deny that fact and save himself? Peter listened closely.

"I am." Peter could hear Jesus' ringing voice, calm and firm and clear.

The crowd seemed to go mad. Through the courtyard window Peter could see them strike Jesus. He could see them spit upon him and beat him. Yet Jesus answered nothing.

Peter shivered as he drew near to the fire and spread his hands before the blaze. Around

him were the servants of the high priest and the mob who had come to the arrest of Jesus.

As he mingled with them, the maid who had opened the door saw him.

"This man was with Jesus of Galilee," she said, pointing to Peter.

Peter was afraid, dreadfully afraid. "I don't even know him," he replied.

The girl said no more. Peter drew nearer to the warmth. As he did so, the firelight fell on his face, and one of the men exclaimed:

"This man also was with Jesus, the Nazarene!"

"I do not know him," Peter said. And this time he shouted the words.

The crowd was watching him, watching the stranger who warmed himself at the high priest's fire. Another servant entered, one who had been with the mob at the arrest of Jesus. He heard Peter's denial and turned to look at him.

"Of course he is one of them," he said. Then, to Peter, "Did I not see you in the garden with him?"

All of the rough fisherman's speech which he had used on the sea rushed to Peter's lips. "I know him not," he cried.

It was almost morning. As Peter spoke there was the sound of a cock crowing. Peter started up from the seat. As he did so, the door of the inner room opened and the soldiers led Jesus across the courtyard, on his way to be tried by Caiaphas. Jesus looked straight into the eyes of Peter. Then Peter remembered, remembered that Jesus had said, "Before the cock crow this day, thou shalt deny me thrice." And Peter went out and wept bitterly.

But Jesus did not falter. Judas had betrayed him. The other disciples had deserted him. Peter had denied him. But Jesus went on quietly, bravely, to face the Jewish and the Roman courts.

On Calvary

It was early morning in Jerusalem. The streets of the city were crowded. Already the news had spread that Jesus had been arrested in the night; that he had been before the Jewish court and even now was in the palace of Pilate, the Roman governor.

The curious thronged about Pilate's door. Some there were who were more than curious; some were there who loved Jesus. They had arrived in time to hear the mob cry, "Crucify him! Crucify him!"

"Surely," they had thought, "Pilate will not consent."

They had strained their ears to hear the verdict and had started back as Pilate pronounced the sentence of death by crucifixion, at Calvary, the place of execution outside the city walls.

For hours they waited. At last the great doors opened and Jesus appeared. He had been terribly whipped before he was delivered up to be crucified. The hours of strain during the trial, the scourging and mockings after the sentence, had left their mark. There was suffering and sorrow on his face; but there was strength and love, and courage, too.

Bearing his heavy cross, as prisoners did in those days, Jesus passed through the street that is now called "The Way of Sorrow." With him were two robbers who had received the same sentence. With him were the Roman soldiers whose business it was to carry out the governor's commands.

The company halted for a moment. Jesus had stumbled and fallen under the weight of the heavy cross. Hastily the soldiers pressed into service Simon, a man of Cyrene. He lifted the cross from the tired shoulders of Jesus and took it upon his own.

The procession went on—on down the narrow streets and out through the city gate, out toward Calvary.

There, according to their custom, the soldiers offered to each of the condemned, wine mingled with myrrh to deaden the pain. But Jesus did not drink of it.

There on the hill they crucified Jesus and the

two robbers, one on either side of him. No word did Jesus say as the nails were driven into his hands and into his feet. No outcry did he make as the cross was lifted up and steadied into the earth.

The friends who had followed were listening. Would he speak? Then they heard:

"Father, forgive them for they know not what they do!"

The robbers heard that, too.

"Are you the Christ? Then save yourself and us," taunted one of them. But the other shook his head.

"Can you not see that he is different from us?" he said to his companion. "We deserve this punishment, but he has done nothing wrong. Only

God could bear this suffering as he is doing."

Then he said to Jesus:

"Remember me when you come into your kingdom."

Never had Jesus failed one who asked help. He did not fail, even then.

"Truly I tell you," he said, "today thou shalt be with me in Paradise."

Another group, too, heard Jesus' words, the little group of those who loved him; John, Mary, the mother of Jesus, her sister, and Mary Magdalene. It seemed more than the mother could bear. Of her, too, Jesus thought. Looking down at John, he said to Mary, "He will be a son to you." Then to John, "Take her as thy mother."

Later John did take Mary to his own home and cared for her as if she were his own mother.

There was silence for a while.

So quiet it was that someone heard the whisper, "I thirst."

A soldier dipped a sponge in vinegar and held it to Jesus' lips.

It was mid-afternoon now. Jesus spoke again. "It is finished," he said. Then, "Father, into thy hands I commend my spirit!"

So he laid down his life.

The crowd had watched it all. Now they began to drift slowly away.

One man stood apart from the rest. The Roman captain had watched many men die. He had stood beside Jesus' cross through it all. Now he said, "Truly this Man was the Son of God."

John had watched, too. Did he think of the words which Jesus had spoken—words which John wrote down years later? *I am the good shepherd: the good shepherd giveth his life for his sheep. . . . No man taketh it from me, but I lay it down of myself.*

It was almost sundown, the hour when the Sabbath of the Jews began. Joseph of Arimathaea, a good man, went to the Roman governor,

Pilate, and asked for the body of Jesus that he might bury it. Pilate gave his permission. With Nicodemus's help, Joseph bathed the hurt body and wrapped it in soft linen scented with sweet spices. Then they carried it to Joseph's garden and put it in a new tomb cut in the rocks. They rolled a great stone against the door, and Pilate had the opening sealed with his own seal, for, said the enemies of Jesus, "He said that he would rise from the dead. His disciples might steal the body and say that he did that."

So Pilate placed a guard of soldiers at the tomb of Jesus to make sure that no one broke the seal. Night came down.

A Glad, Glad Day

It was a sad time for the friends of Jesus in Jerusalem and near by, for Jesus was dead.

One day went by. Two days went by. Sunday morning came, the third day since Jesus had been crucified.

In Joseph's garden outside the city there lingered the quietness of the Jewish Sabbath, a quietness broken only by the stir of the olive trees in the morning breeze.

The white flowers of the almond tree had budded and blossomed, and the hard, shriveled brown bulbs, buried in the earth through the winter, had flowered into red lilies. The sun was rising in the eastern sky, shedding its faint pink glow over the garden and lighting the path to Joseph's new tomb.

Friday had been a day of sorrow for all who loved Jesus. Some had watched him die on the cross. Others had followed as Joseph of Arimathaea and Nicodemus had prepared the body for burial and carried it to the tomb. They had seen the great stone rolled into the door of the tomb. Then they had gone away to mourn. Jesus was dead. His friends heard of the Roman seal Pilate had placed on the tomb and of the soldiers put there to guard it. Saturday came, the Sabbath of the Jews. The long hours dragged slowly by.

Early Sunday morning three women walked quietly through the lonely streets of the city and out to the garden where Jesus was buried.

The preparations for the burial had been hasty, and these three were bringing the spices with which those of the East care for the bodies of their dead. "Who shall roll away the stone from the door of the tomb?" the women asked. As they neared the tomb, they saw that their question needed no answer. The stone had been rolled away. The

women stopped in amazement. Then they went into the tomb. It was empty. As they looked closer they saw near the door a young man clothed in shining white.

"Why seek ye the living among the dead?" the angel asked. "Jesus is not here. He is risen even as he said. Come, see the place where the Lord lay."

The women looked.

There were the clothes lying neatly at one side. There was the empty tomb.

"Do you not remember," the angel questioned, "how he said, 'The Son of man must be delivered into the hands of sinful men and be crucified, and the third day rise again'?"

The women had forgotten.

The angel spoke to them again, "Go tell his disciples—and Peter. He will meet them in Galilee."

It was later near the tomb that Mary heard a voice speaking by her side. "Why are you crying?"

"It must be the gardener," Mary thought. And she did not lift her eyes.

"Tell me," she said, "where is the body of

Jesus?" For Mary could not yet believe that he had risen from the dead.

"Mary!"

It was the voice she loved best of all.

"Jesus! Master!"

Mary had turned and was kneeling at Jesus' feet.

"Mary," Jesus spoke again, "go tell my disciples." And Mary hastened back to Jerusalem with the glad, glad news that the Lord was risen from the dead.

For forty days Jesus walked the roads and streets of Jerusalem just as he used to do. The disciples saw him. Peter saw him. Two friends walked down the road to Emmaus with him one day and knew him as he broke bread with them and gave thanks. Many other of his friends saw him. The gladness of his rising spread all the time.

The Lord of All

Everywhere Jesus' friends began to hear the glad news that he was alive. It was hard to believe. One afternoon there were seven disciples together. There were Peter, Thomas, John, and James and three more of Jesus' disciple friends. All of them were sad.

"We do miss Jesus so much," one of the disciple friends sighed. "We are lonesome without him."

The others shook their heads slowly.

"Some people say we will never see Jesus any more," they said. "It is a long time since he went away."

The disciple friends were quiet. The sun had almost set when Peter spoke.

"I am going fishing," Peter said.

The other disciples looked up.

"We will go with you," they told Peter.

One, two, three, four, five, six, seven. There were seven sad men sailing in a little boat out on the blue waters of the lake. Peter and Thomas

were there. James and John were there. There
were three more of Jesus' disciple friends. And
all of them were sad.

The seven sad men fished until the last pink
light from the setting sun was gone. They fished
until the yellow moon came, and the stars were
twinkling in the blue sky. The moon went down.
It was dark.

All night long the seven disciple friends fished.
Over and over again they let their net down into
the water and pulled it up empty. They did not
catch even one fish.

The first light of the rising sun was touching the water when they started for shore.

Suddenly the seven sad men heard a voice.

"Children," someone was calling, "have you any meat?"

The disciple friends looked toward the shore. A man stood there.

The disciple friends shouted their answer.

"No," they shouted, "we have no meat. We have fished all night, and we have not caught even one fish."

The man was speaking again.

"Let down your net on the right side of the

boat," he said. "There you will find fish."

The disciple friends did as they were told.

Down, down, down, they let the net on the right side of the boat. They waited a moment. Then they pulled. The net was heavy with fish!

John thought of a night long ago when Jesus had helped his friends catch fish. John pointed to the shore.

"It is Jesus!" John said. "The man on the shore is Jesus!"

Peter could not wait. Before the others knew what was happening, he had jumped into the water and was swimming to the shore.

The other men lifted the net heavy with fish and began to row the boat. When they got to the shore they saw red coals of fire with fish and bread cooking over them.

"Get some of your fish to cook," Jesus said.

And the disciple friends did. One hundred and fifty-three fish they counted as they emptied the net.

Soon breakfast was ready.

"Come," Jesus said. "It is time to eat."

The disciple friends sat down.

One, two, three, four, five, six, seven, eight.

There were eight glad men together for breakfast that fine morning. Peter and Thomas were glad. James and John were glad. Three other disciples were glad. All of the friends were glad. They no longer were sad.

For one of the men was Jesus.

It was when the meal was finished that Jesus turned to Peter.

"Simon, son of Jonas," he said, "do you love me more than these?" Perhaps Jesus pointed to the net full of fish.

"Yes, Lord; you know that I love you." Peter

could hardly say the words for the memory of those denials on the night of Jesus' arrest choked him.

"Feed my lambs," said Jesus.

Peter was thinking it over. Would Jesus trust him with a task after all that had happened?

Again Jesus asked the question, "Simon, son of Jonas, do you love me?"

"Yes, Lord; you know that I love you." Peter said the words again but this time the reply came more clearly.

"Take care of my sheep," said Jesus.

It is true, thought Peter. He is going to trust me again.

Again Jesus asked the question.

"Simon, son of Jonas, do you love me?"

There was sorrow in Peter's voice as he answered, but of one thing he was very, very sure. "Lord," he said, "you know all things; you know that I love you."

Again came the trust, "Feed my sheep."

He would try, oh! how hard Peter would try to be true to the trust which Jesus was giving him.

"It will not be easy, Peter," Jesus said. "When you were a young man you were a fisherman. You went where you wished. But when you are old, if you are true to my trust, you will be a prisoner. You will be bound and taken to places where you do not want to go."

Jesus told Peter of the hardships. He told him that it was not going to be easy to be true to the trust. But after he told him, there came the old invitation in the same words Peter had heard months before, by the seaside, "Follow me."

And Peter with heart overflowing in gratitude for his second chance, did follow. He followed Jesus to the end of his days.

And so the friends of Jesus came to understand

that death had not taken their Lord from them. He was living, real, their Friend and Helper, just as he had always been. The Lord Jesus was expecting them to carry on his work of spreading the news of God and his way of love. He was depending upon them to preach the gospel. Jesus told them about it one day.

"All power is given unto me in heaven and on earth," Jesus said. "Go into all the world and tell people about me. Go to all lands. Preach the gospel to red and yellow people. Preach it to black and white people. Preach the gospel of God's love to all people. Teach them to do all the things I have commanded you. And lo, I am with you always, even unto the end of the world."

One day Jesus led his disciples out through the streets of Jerusalem to the hill of Olivet that looked down on the village of Bethany. At the top of the hill they stopped and rested, and Jesus talked to his friends about the things he wanted them to do. Then he lifted his hands and blessed them.

And even as he spoke, a cloud hid him from their sight, and the Lord Jesus was carried up into heaven.

As the disciples stood looking up, they saw two men in shining white garments.

"Why do you stand gazing into heaven?" these men said. "This same Jesus whom you have seen go away shall come again."

The disciples praised God. Then, joyfully, they returned to Jerusalem. Everywhere they went, they told the good news of the Lord Jesus. They told the glad news of God and his love.

But no one could ever tell all the wonderful things Jesus did. No book could ever hold all the stories about him. Jesus' friend, John, knew that. In his own story of Jesus, he said that if all the things Jesus did were told, "even the world itself could not contain the books that should be written."

It was long ago in the land of Palestine that John wrote those words. And even today all over the world people are writing about Jesus. This book has tried to tell the stories that Matthew and Mark and Luke and John wrote down in the Bible.

They are stories of the living Lord who is stronger than death, stories of One who came to tell people about God and his love, stories of the Man who went about doing good, stories of God's Son who came to be the Saviour-helper to all who trust him, stories of the Baby of whom the angel said:

"Thou shalt call his name Jesus."